Praise for
The Road to Assisi

"This new and updated edition . . . is nothing short of astonishing in its power to touch the heart and revive the soul." —*St. Anthony Messenger*

"This book brings forth this popular saint in a way in which we come to know him more intimately than ever before. Everyone touched by this 'perpetual outsider' will want to read it." —M. Basil Pennington, O.C.S.O.

"*The Road to Assisi* . . . offers an excellent introduction to the text, helpful sidebars and notes, and fascinating illustrations, [aiding readers] in engaging 'personally with Francis, the human being.'" —*Publishers Weekly*

"Paul Sabatier's groundbreaking 1894 biography *Vie de S. François d'Assise* is essential reading for anyone interested in the life and times of the great charismatic of Assisi. *The Road to Assisi* offers a clear and temperate introduction to Sabatier's passionate, often controversial engagement with the radical life and message of St. Francis. Highly recommended." —Valerie Martin, author of *Salvation: Scenes from the Life of St. Francis.*

"Today, under the editorial guidance of Sweeney, this balanced, long-out-of-print work is again in the hands of readers." —*Library Journal*

"Sabatier's 19th century biography still reads like the classic it is. One could hardly ask for a better combination to introduce Francis to a larger public."—Mark Galli, author of *Francis and His World* and managing editor for *Christianity Today*

"[This] remarkable new publication from Paraclete Press has something to say to you . . . a refreshing and eye-opening work." —*The Episcopal New Yorker*

"*The Road to Assisi* presents Sabatier's biography for today's reader. With helpful explanations and annotations by Jon M. Sweeney, Sabatier's narrative is supplemented with the insights of many other scholars and writers." —*The Presbyterian Outlook*

Jon M. Sweeney is an author and editor recognized for his ability to communicate religious and theological ideas in uncomplicated language. He is the editor-in-chief of Skylight Paths Publishing and the author of *Praying With Our Hands: 21 Practices of Embodied Prayer from the World's Spiritual Traditions* and the *St. Francis Prayer Book: A Guide to Deepen Your Spiritual Life*. His work has appeared in various magazines, including *The Lutheran, Spirituality & Health, The Merton Seasonal,* and *Sacred Journey.* Sweeney lives in a log cabin in Vermont, with his wife, Danelle Sims Sweeney, and their two children.

Paul Sabatier (1858-1928) was raised in the Cevennes, a mountainous region of southern France, educated in Paris, and served as pastor in Strasbourg. In mid-life, he dedicated the rest of his life to research and writing. His life of Francis, *Vie de S. François d'Assise,* was first published in 1894 and then quickly translated into English, Swedish, German, and Italian. Within a few years, it was a bestseller around the world. Sabatier's pioneering work has influenced, and made possible, the work of generations of scholars and biographers since his time.

THE
ROAD
TO
ASSISI

The Essential Biography of St. Francis

PAUL SABATIER

EDITED WITH INTRODUCTION
AND ANNOTATIONS BY JON M. SWEENEY

PARACLETE PRESS
BREWSTER, MASSACHUSETTS

2005 Second Trade Paperback Printing
2004 First Trade Paperback Printing
2003 First Hardcover Printing

© 2003 by Jon M. Sweeney

ISBN: 1-55725-401-X

Scripture quotations are taken from the New Revised Standard Version of the Bible, copyright 1989, Division of Christian Education of the National Council of the Churches of Christ in the U.S.A. All rights reserved. Used by permission.

Library of Congress Cataloging-in-Publication Data
Sabatier, Paul, 1858–1928.
    The road to Assisi : the essential biography of St. Francis / by Paul Sabatier ; edited with introduction and annotations by Jon M. Sweeney.
        p. cm.
    ISBN 1-55725-401-x
1. Francis, of Assisi, Saint, 1182-1226. 2. Christian saints—Italy—Biography. I. Sweeney, Jon M., 1967 – II. Title.
    BX4700.F6S19 2003
    271'.302—dc21

                                                                    2003002011

10 9 8 7 6 5 4 3 2

Published by Paraclete Press
Brewster, Massachusetts
www.paracletepress.com

Printed in the United States of America.

For Sarah-Maria and Joseph,
the spirit of St. Francis.

And to Danelle,
for everything.

—J.M.S.

CONTENTS

INTRODUCTION

Paul Sabatier (1858–1928) was the first modern biographer of St. Francis of Assisi. A French Protestant, Sabatier was motivated to write about the saint out of love for his unusual and creative life.

It can be a very personal and moving experience to write about the little poor man from Umbria. Over the centuries, many authors have been profoundly affected as they have "lived" with Francis while recounting his life. Nikos Kazantzakis, the twentieth-century Greek novelist, said that, while writing his novel *Saint Francis,* "often large teardrops smeared the manuscript."

It is not simply that Francis's ideals are worth recounting, but that his life was so extraordinary. He was fully human—like each of us in our awkwardness, insecurities, and fear—but he was also perhaps the purest example we have seen of a person striving to do what Jesus taught his disciples.

To write about Francis is to wish the same courage and heart into ourselves. This wishing—these good intentions—are often the stuff of our spiritual lives, as perhaps when we touch an icon, or wake up early before the rest of the house is awake to pray in solitude, or when we truly hunger for righteousness, as many of our liturgies say. Reading and writing about Francis can be our attempt, like a medium or sacrament, to enlarge our own capacities to be like him.

Paul Sabatier was born in the Cevennes, a mountainous region of southern France, in August 1858. He was educated in theology in Paris and after preparing for the ministry became pastor of St. Nicolas, Strasbourg, a post he held until he was almost forty. After a brief sojourn as pastor of St. Cierge back in the Cevennes he then devoted the rest of his life to historical writing and research. His book, *Vie de S. François d'Assise,* was first published in French in 1894. Thirty-two years later, a scholar of Franciscan studies wrote: "Countless thousands of readers have derived from . . . Sabatier . . . their first impulse towards interest in the saint, which has frequently developed into a complete surrender to his fascination and charm" (Seton, p. 252).

Sabatier's brother, the more famous of the two men, was old enough to be his father. Louis Auguste Sabatier (1839–1901) was a theologian and professor of dogmatics in the theology department at the University of Strasbourg and, later, was a member of the newly formed Protestant faculty in Paris. A Huguenot, Auguste found that his loyalty to French causes ultimately led to his being forced by the Germans to leave Strasbourg in the early 1870s. About fifteen years later, Paul Sabatier also fell out of favor with his German superiors, declining to become a German citizen, and left his pulpit in Strasbourg only to return in 1919 as a professor of church history. He dedicated his book on Francis to the people of Strasbourg. However, we might thank the Germans for forcing Sabatier into retirement from the active ministry (he was also plagued by health problems), leaving him the freedom and time to live in Italy, to do research, and to write his great biography.

Sabatier was moved by Francis, the man, and he wanted to create the first telling of his life that reflected the possibilities afforded by modern scholarship. He was the first person to scour the libraries of Italy to uncover original documents, and he employed textual and historical criticism as well as psychological insight. Modern scholarship, so-called, was new in Sabatier's time, in the second half of the nineteenth century. As a student, Sabatier listened to the lectures of the dynamic historian and critic Ernest Renan (1823–1892). It was Renan's groundbreaking—or notorious, depending on your perspective—work exposing naïveté in most precritical studies of the historical Jesus that motivated Sabatier to write his modern life of Francis, looking for the man amidst the layers of myth and legend. It was Renan who said: "No miracle has ever taken place under conditions that science can accept. Experience shows, without exception, that miracles occur only in times and in countries in which miracles are believed in, and in the presence of persons who are disposed to believe in them." Renan's book *Vie de Jésus* was published only thirty years before Sabatier's life of Francis; comparisons between the two works were inevitable. "So the sensation of delight or anger with which [Sabatier's] book was received is easy to explain" (BPL, p. 274).

These were the heady, early days of ultimate confidence in the power of science and logic to make faith unnecessary. But Sabatier did not follow Renan in discarding the reality of the mysterious. (Renan, for instance, explained Francis's stigmata as a deliberate hoax perpetuated by Brother Elias.) He did, however, accept the basic notion that many things can be seen only with eyes of faith; many realities may be understood only with a heart disposed to realize them.

Sabatier believed that to deny all of the miraculous in the lives of the saints was to deny a life-transforming faith. In the introduction to the first edition of his life of Francis, he separated himself from Renan, his teacher, when he wrote the following:

> Happily we are no longer in the time when historians thought they had done the right thing when they had reduced everything to its proper size, contenting themselves with denying or omitting everything in the life of the heroes of humanity that rises above the level of our everyday experiences.
>
> No doubt Francis did not meet on the road to Siena three pure and gentle virgins come from heaven to greet him; the devil did not overturn rocks for the sake of terrifying him; but when we deny these visions and apparitions, we are victims of an error graver, perhaps, than that of those who affirm them (SABATIER, p. XXX).

Sabatier's book was first published in French in 1894 (although early copies were distributed in the closing months of 1893), and quickly became a bestseller, almost unheard of for a work of its kind in those days. English, Swedish, German, and Italian editions followed within the next several years. When Sabatier died in the spring of 1928, forty-five editions had been published in the French language alone.

Scholarly reaction to the book was immediate and, most of it, favorable. Sabatier was quickly seen as one of his generation's most important historians. Both Catholics and Protestants admired the work, but the official Roman Catholic response was to condemn it. Historical and textual criticism applied to the legends of the saints was not looked upon favorably at the close of the nineteenth century. The book made the infamous Roman "Index" (*Index*

Librorum Prohibitorum) of forbidden books in the same year that it was first published.

Catholic authorities saw too much of a rebel in Sabatier's portrait of Francis. Always careful to portray this—the greatest of saints of the people—as a supporter of the Church, its doctrine, and hierarchy, popes and other staunch protectors of the faith have often proclaimed: "How foolish they are, and how little they know the saint of Assisi, who for the purpose of their own errors invent a Francis—an incredible Francis—who is impatient of the authority of the Church. . . . Let [Francis], the herald of the great King, teach Catholics and others by his own example how close was his attachment to the hierarchy of the Church and to the doctrines of Christ" (Encyclical Letter of Pope Pius XI, written in 1926 for the 700th anniversary of the saint's death; see SETON, p. 251).

Sabatier certainly shows us a Francis who is often going his own way. However, he is also careful to show both sides of the story, as when he wrote this passage: "One of Francis's most frequent counsels bore upon the respect due to the clergy. He begged his disciples to show a very particular deference to the priests, and never to meet them without kissing their hands. He saw only too well that the brothers, having renounced everything, were in danger of being unjust or severe toward the rich and powerful of the earth" (SABATIER, pp. 168–69).

As is true of any great work, Sabatier's life of Francis has given birth to hundreds of others, and also has enlightened his critics. Since the closing years of the nineteenth century there has been appreciation for Sabatier's book, but plenty of criticism as well. Many Franciscan scholars have disagreed with some of his conclusions, primarily the subtle ways in which the French Protestant portrays Francis as a forerunner of the Protestant Reformation of the sixteenth century. Other scholarly reactions have ranged widely. For instance, while some reviewers have deplored Sabatier's critical stance in reference to the Francis legends—thinking it wrong to view a medieval saint through a modern lens—others, including the popular medieval scholar and sometime critic of institutional religion G. G. Coulton, have taken Sabatier, his contemporary, to task for not being critical enough, for continuing to perpetuate credulity.

Sabatier's Francis is a gentle mystic and passionate reformer guided by an unwavering vision of fulfilling the ideals of Christ: the brotherhood of all people, evangelical poverty, and forgiveness, all with a Christ-filled intoxicating joy. An anti-intellectual at heart, Sabatier's Francis confounds the wise with his clarity of vision and dedicated praxis, and even occasionally by his holy foolishness. In Sabatier's book, the simple beauty of Francis's life and message is set clearly against the obscuring of that message in the years following the saint's death. The narrative builds to, and reveals, this eventual sadness. Francis the prophet is set against the priests of his day, and even against many of the Franciscan brothers and priests that followed in his footsteps.

Contemporary theologian Lawrence Cunningham writes: "Sabatier's mentor, Renan, once quipped that Jesus preached the Kingdom of God and the world ended up with the Catholic Church. Sabatier's biography was a variation on this theme: Francis had preached a lay Christianity bent on radical spiritual renewal, and Europe ended up with the Franciscan order" (CUNNINGHAM 1, pp. 865–68).

Sabatier also portrays Francis as an important forerunner of the Italian Renaissance. The "birth of the individual," long recognized as one of the key signposts of the Renaissance, is exemplified in the life of Francis. One Dutch scholar summarizes this, saying: "Perhaps Sabatier has contributed more than anyone to the shift in the nature and the dating of the concept of the Renaissance. It was no longer a growth of the mind . . . but a growth of the heart: the opening of the eyes and the soul to all the excellence of the world and the individual personality" (HUIZINGA, pp. 263–64).

Jacob Burckhardt, renowned historian of the Italian Renaissance, wrote a generation before Sabatier: "At the close of the thirteenth century Italy began to swarm with individuality; the ban laid upon human personality was dissolved; and a thousand figures meet us each in its own special shape and dress" (BURCKHARDT, p. 81). Burckhardt, however, does not in his secularism credit the revolution of spirit brought about by Francis with sparking a new individuality; for Burckhardt, the emergence of the individual in the early Renaissance period was the result, above all, of political change.

In his perspective on the life of Francis, Sabatier stood some-where between the dry academics—Renan and Matthew Arnold, for instance, writing in the decades before Sabatier—and the absolutely devoted—Thomas of Celano, St. Bonaventure, and the other hagio-graphic and piously written "lives" of the saint. Since minutes after Francis's death—when the canonization process began in earnest and Assisi was quickly established as one of the most important places for tourism and pilgrimage in all of Christendom—until the late nineteenth century, the life of Francis was clouded in myth. *The Golden Legend*, a popular late medieval collection of tales from the lives of the saints, for instance, records this about Francis: "The saint would not handle lanterns and lamps and candles because he did not want to dim their brightness with his hands." Also: "A locust that nested in a fig tree next to his cell used to sing at all hours, until the man of God extended his hand and said: 'My sister locust, come here to me!' Obediently the locust came up and rested on his hand. 'My sister locust, sing! Sing, and praise your Lord!' The locust began to sing and did not hop away until the saint gave permission" (VORAGINE, p. 225).

Tellingly, Thomas of Celano, the first biographer of Francis, wrote in the prologue to his first life of the saint, "Pious devotion and truth will always be my guide and instructor" (ARMSTRONG, p. 180). Before Sabatier, historical evidence and hagiography were necessarily intertwined.

It is also important to realize, before reading Sabatier's book, that he stood in a long line of speculative Protestant tradition rich with disdain, even sarcasm, for the lives of the saints. For example, one popular Protestant book of the seventeenth century recounts "miracle" after "miracle" of Francis and the Franciscans only to show their ultimate foolishness. One sample miracle account reads this way:

> Frier Francis, in celebrating of mass, found a Spider in the Cup, which he would not cast away, but drank it off with the bloud, afterwards scratching his thigh, where he felt it itch, the Spider came out of his thigh without hurting the Frier.

And the interpretation reads this way:

Knave might have let this lie alone, for a Spider is not such poyson, as to deserve such a lie: For a cup of strong Wine without a Miracle is antidote enough against one (ALCORAN, pp. 59–60).

G. K. Chesterton, whose own book on Francis shows a deep level of personal understanding of his life, summarizes the many possible perspectives from which to write a modern life of St. Francis. Contrasting the viewpoints of the academics with those of the faithful, he writes: "A materialist may not care whether the inconsistencies are reconciled or not. A Catholic may not see any inconsistencies to reconcile." In his book, Chesterton opts for a perspective that is "sympathetic but skeptical," an approach similar to that of Sabatier.

Clearly, Sabatier loved his subject. But also as clearly, Sabatier was a thoroughly modern man who wanted to satisfy his own modern curiosities about miracles, influences, and conflict in Francis's life. The result is an engaging and fascinating portrait. Whereas, as Chesterton says—"Renan and Matthew Arnold were content to follow Francis with their praises until they were stopped by their prejudices"—Sabatier follows our subject throughout his extraordinary life, in all of its perplexities. It is Sabatier's passion for Francis that reassures us as we read his critical approach to the saint's life.

Sabatier became the leader, after a decade or so of mixed reaction, of a renaissance of interest in Francis. He corresponded with hundreds of students, readers, and scholars in several languages. He spent his last years back in the Cevennes in a villa near Chabrillanoux. At Sabatier's death in 1928, the Boston Public Library purchased his library from his widow. The 1931 volume of *More Books: The Bulletin of the Boston Public Library* announced the addition of the collection, summarizing the importance of Sabatier's *Life of St. Francis of Assisi*:

Sabatier's book brought back the reality of the "Little Poor Man" to multitudes. Once more, that strange figure in a small Italian town, who took upon himself to live the life of Christ and who succeeded in it better than any other person before or since, was before the public. Instead of the founder of a religious Order, Francis of Assisi became again "the jongleur of God"; a man who hated money and all other possessions, who prostrated himself before the meanest leper—who was so drunken with love and compassion for Christ that he could not distinguish his joy from his tears (BPL, p. 273).

No reader will understand the life of St. Francis without first understanding that religion—especially Francis's very personal faith—is to be understood intimately. Again, to use a phrase from Chesterton (because he is so accurate in these matters), "it is only the most personal passion that provides here an approximate earthly parallel" to understanding the life of Francis.

The primary difficulty that remains for any reader about to encounter Francis for the first time is this: Was Francis *real* in the sense that his life can have any relationship to the meaning of my own? I hope, at least for my own sake, that the answer is increasingly "yes." Francis's spirit lives on in extraordinary people today. Standing as we do with the benefit of hindsight, the similarities between the little poor man from Assisi and other notable spiritual figures, such as Mahatma Gandhi, for instance, are many. Despite different religious underpinnings, we can almost see Francis when we see photographs of the sandled, loin-clothed Gandhi negotiating with the rulers of Europe. In other contexts, Francis has been compared to Dorothy Day, founder of the Catholic Worker movement in twentieth-century America, and Mother Teresa of Calcutta, just to name a few. We each have the capacity to be a saint like him; Francis certainly believed so.

I hope that this book will serve as an informational and engaging introduction to the life of St. Francis for the reader interested in his life for the first time. But more important, I hope that *The Road to Assisi* will be a vehicle for you, the reader, to engage personally with Francis, the human being. As Nikos Kazantzakis summarized the meaning of Francis's life in the Prologue to his novel on the saint, each of us has "the obligation to transubstantiate the matter which God entrusted to us, and turn it into spirit."

What keeps the life and message of St. Francis from moving us to action? What keeps it from moving me to action, to change my life to be more like him? These questions are similar to those of art historian James Elkins, in the preface to his engaging book *Pictures & Tears*. Elkins wants to understand why art does not more easily "move" us. Allow me to quote one long paragraph in conclusion, with the hope that the parallels will be obvious:

> Our lack of intensity [in viewing paintings] is a fascinating problem. I'd like to understand why it seems normal to look at astonishing achievements made by unapproachably ambitious, luminously pious, strangely obsessed artists, and toss them off with a few wry comments. . . . What does it mean to say that you love paintings (and even spend your life living among them, as professionals do) and still feel so little? If paintings are so important—worth so much, reproduced, cherished, and visited so often—then isn't it troubling that we can hardly make emotional contact with them? (ELKINS, p. IX)

THE
ANNOTATED LIFE
OF
ST. FRANCIS OF ASSISI

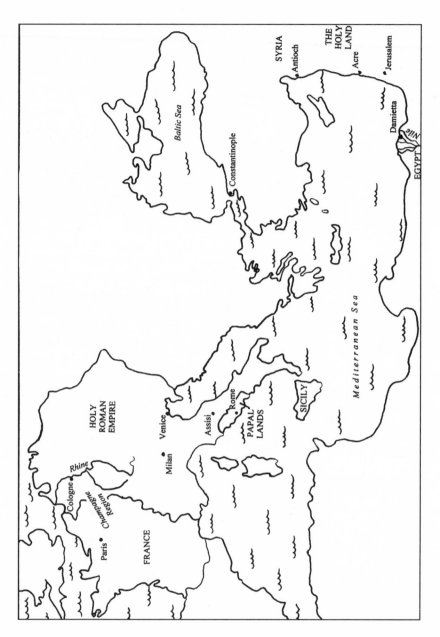

Italy, Central Europe, and The Holy Land ca. 1200 C.E.

CHAPTER ONE
His Youth and Family

Assisi is today very much what it was six or seven hundred years ago. The feudal castle is in ruins, but the aspect of the city is just the same. Its long-deserted streets, bordered by ancient houses, lie in terraces halfway up the steep hillside. Above it Mount Subasio proudly towers, at its feet lies outspread all the Umbrian plain from Perugia to Spoleto. The crowded houses clamber up the rocks like children a-tiptoe to see all that is to be seen; they succeed so well that every window gives the whole panorama set in its frame of rounded hills, from the summits of which castles and villages stand sharply out against a sky of incomparable purity.

He was born about 1182. The biographies have preserved to us few details about his parents. His father, Peter Bernardone, was a wealthy cloth-merchant. We know how different was the life of the merchants of that period from what it is today. A great portion of their time was spent in extensive journeys for the purchase of goods. Such tours were little short of expeditions. The roads being insecure, a strong escort was needed for the journey to those famous fairs where, for long weeks at a time, merchants from the most remote parts of Europe were gathered together.

Sabatier's life of Francis was originally published in 1894. If written today, his first sentence would read: "Assisi is today very much what it was more than eight hundred years ago."

The original Assisan castle was built around the time of Charlemagne, who first razed, and then rebuilt, Assisi. When Francis was a teenager, a horde of Assisans stormed the castle, associated as it was with despotic power (whoever invaded or ruled Assisi took possession of it), and destroyed most of it. One hundred and seventy years later, the new rocca was completed. The castle was once called Rocca d'Assisi, the fortress of Assisi, and today, Rocca Maggiore ("larger castle").

Mount Subasio (4,230 ft.) gives foundation to the ancient city of Assisi. Most of the beautiful pink, grey, and white limestone of the Assisan buildings was originally quarried from Subasio. A national park sits atop Subasio today; tourists often climb to the top for the spectacular views.

Among all these merchants the richest were those who dealt in textile stuffs. They were literally the bankers of the time, and their heavy wagons were often laden with the sums levied by the popes in England or France. Bernardone often made these long journeys; he went even as far as France, and by this we must surely understand Northern France, and particularly Champagne, which was the seat of commercial exchange between Northern and Southern Europe.

He was not there at the very time of his son's birth. The mother, presenting the child at the font of San Rufino, had him baptized by the name of John, but the father on his return chose to call him Francis. Perhaps, indeed, the name was only a sort of grateful homage tendered by the Assisan burgher to his noble clients beyond the Alps.

Merchants, indeed, played a considerable part in the religious movements of the thirteenth century. Their calling in some sense forced them to become colporters of ideas. What else could they do, on arriving in a country, but answer those who asked for news? And the news most eagerly looked for was religious news, for people's minds were turned upon very different subjects than they are now. They accommodated themselves to the popular wish, observing, hearkening everywhere, keeping eyes and ears open, glad to find anything to tell, and little by little many of them became active propagandists of ideas concerning which at first they had been simply curious.

The importance of the part played by the merchants as they came

Not all of the medieval popes were located in Rome. From 1309 to 1377, the kings of England and France defied the Church in Rome and established a succession of seven popes who ruled from Avignon, in France. This was followed by "The Great Schism," when, from 1378 to 1417, two, and during one period, three, popes ruled, supported by differing factions of the Church.

Champagne is not just a bubbly wine. (Although it was at the Abbey of Saint-Pierre, in the province of Champagne, that Dom Perignon, Benedictine monk, invented bottled champagne in the early 1700s.) Champagne became a part of France about 90 years after Francis's death. As Sabatier mentions, for almost 200 years, beginning around 1150—or, at about the time of Peter Bernardone's birth—Champagne was the international center of European trade. Not far from Paris to the west, or the German cities of Mainz and Cologne to the east, the province of Champagne in northeastern France also sat strategically on the main north-south trade route between Flanders, on the North Sea, and the cities in the north of Italy. Merchants would gather from all over Europe, guaranteed safe travel by the counts of Champagne, to trade with each other; these sessions would last for as long as two months at a stretch.

and went, everywhere sowing the new ideas that they had gathered up in their travels, has not been put in a clear enough light. They were often, unconsciously and quite involuntarily, the carriers of ideas of all kinds, especially of heresy and rebellion. It was they who made the success of the Waldensians, the Albigensians, the Humiliati, and many other sects.

Thus Bernardone, without dreaming of such a thing, became the artisan of his son's religious vocation. The tales that he brought home from his travels seemed at first, perhaps, not to have aroused the child's attention, but they were like germs a long time buried, which suddenly, under a warm ray of sunlight, bring forth unlooked-for fruit.

The boy's education was not carried very far; the school was in those days overshadowed by the church. The priests of San Giorgio were his teachers, and they taught him a little Latin. This language was spoken in Umbria until toward the middle of the thirteenth century; every one understood it and spoke it a little; it was still the language of sermons and of political deliberations.

He learned also to write, but with less success; all through his life we see him take up the pen only on rare occasions, and for but a few words. In general he dictated, signing his letters by a simple T, the symbol of the cross of Jesus.

The part of his education destined to have the most influence on his life was the French language, which he may have spoken in his family. It has been rightly said that to know two languages is to have two souls. In learning the language of France the boy felt his heart thrill to the melody of its youthful poetry, and his imagination was mysteriously stirred with dreams of imitating the exploits of the French cavaliers.

His father's profession and the possibly noble origin of his mother raised him almost to the level of the titled families of the country. Money, which he spent with both hands, made him welcome among them. Pleased to enjoy themselves at his expense, the young nobles paid him a sort of court. As to Bernardone, he was too happy to see his son associating with them to be overly concerned as to the means. He was miserly, as the course of this story will show, but his pride and self-conceit exceeded his avarice.

Pica, his wife, a gentle and modest woman, about whom the biographers have always been too silent, would not despair of her son. When the neighbors told her of Francis's escapades, she would calmly reply: "I am very sure that, if it pleases God, Francis will become a good Christian." The words were natural enough from a mother's lips, but later on they were held to have been truly prophetic.

The son of Bernardone not only patterned himself after the young men of his age, he made it a point of honor to exceed them. With eccentricities, buffooneries, pranks, and prodigalities, he ended by achieving a sort of celebrity. He was forever in the streets with his companions, compelling attention by his extravagant or fantastic attire. Even at night the joyous company kept up their merrymakings, causing the town to ring with their noisy songs.

At this very time the troubadours were roaming over the towns of northern Italy and bringing brilliant festivities and especially Courts of Love into vogue. If they worked upon the passions, they also appealed to feelings of courtesy and delicacy; it was this that saved Francis. In the midst of his excesses he was always refined and considerate, carefully abstaining from every base or indecent utterance.

Already his chief aspiration was to rise above the commonplace. Tortured with the desire for that which is far off and high, he had conceived a sort of passion for chivalry, and fancying that dissipation was one of the distinguishing features of nobility, he had thrown himself into it with all his soul.

But he who, at twenty, goes from pleasure to pleasure with the heart not absolutely closed to good, must now and then, at some turning of the road, become aware that there are hungry folk who could live a month on what he spends in a few hours on frivolity. Francis saw them, and with his impressionable nature for the moment forgot everything else. In thought he put himself in their place, and it sometimes happened that he gave them all the money he had about him and even his clothes.

One day he was busy with some customers in his father's shop, when a man came in, begging for charity in the name of God. Losing his patience Francis sharply turned him away; but quickly reproaching himself for his harshness he thought, "What would I not have done if this man had asked something of me in the name of a count or a baron? What ought I not to have done when he came in the name of God? I am no better than a clown!" Leaving his customers he ran after the beggar.

Bernardone had been pleased with his son's commercial aptitude in the early days when the young man was first in his father's employ. Francis was only too proficient in spending money, but at least he knew well how to make it. But this satisfaction did not last long. Francis's companions were exercising a most pernicious influence over him. The time came when he could no longer endure to be separated from them; if he heard their call, nothing could keep him; he would leave everything and go after them.

St. Bonaventure (c. 1220–1274), the most important of the second generation of Franciscans, adds this to the story: "But speedily recollecting himself, (Francis) ran after the poor man, charitably relieved his wants, and made a solemn promise to God that, from that day forth, he would never refuse alms to any that should ask them of him for the love of God."

All this time political events were hurrying on in Umbria and Italy. The rivalries between cities were strong, and Perugia, Assisi's neighbor to the west, was at this time at the apogee of its power, having already made many efforts to reduce Assisi to submission. It declared war on Assisi in 1202. An encounter took place in the plain about halfway between the two cities, not far from *Ponte San Giovanni*. Assisi was defeated, and Francis, who was in the ranks, was made prisoner.

The treachery of the nobles was not universal; a few had fought along with the people. It was with them and not with the *popolani* ("common people") that Francis, in consideration of the nobility of his manners, passed the time of his captivity, which lasted an entire year. He greatly astonished his companions by his lightness of heart. Very often they thought him almost crazy. Instead of passing his time in wailing and cursing he made plans for the future, about which he was glad to talk to any one who came along. His fancy life was something that the songs of the troubadours had painted; he dreamed of glorious adventures, and always ended by saying: "You will see that one day I shall be adored by the whole world."

A compromise was finally arrived at between the counts and the people of Assisi. The agreement being made, the prisoners detained at Perugia were released, and Francis returned to Assisi. He was twenty-two years old.

Francis later turned his secular passion for the poetry of the troubadours to God's service. "All through the thirteenth [century], we find an increasing flood of popular religious works, competing...directly with the ordinary minstrel.... St. Francis had told his disciples to be God's gleemen—joculatores Dei. He himself is recorded to have preached one of his most remarkable sermons from the text of a French love-song: and one of his early disciples, Brother Henry of Pisa, resolved that 'the Devil should not have all the best tunes', and turned current love-songs into hymns" (COULTON, p. 529).

The two cities of Perugia and Assisi are only sixteen miles apart, separated by the Tiber River, which, in ancient times, also divided the Roman and Etruscan empires. Even today, different dialects are nurtured in Perugia and Assisi, even though the Romans defeated the Etruscans in 283 B.C.E.

CHAPTER TWO

Stages of Conversion
(Spring 1204–Spring 1206)

On his return to Assisi Francis at once resumed his former mode of life; perhaps he even tried in some degree to make up for lost time. Fetes, games, festivals, and dissipations began again. He did his part in them so well that he soon fell gravely ill. For long weeks he looked death so closely in the face that the physical crisis brought about a moral one.

Thomas of Celano (a companion of Francis who was also his first biographer) has preserved for us an incident of Francis's convalescence. He was regaining strength little by little and had begun to go about the house, when one day he felt a desire to walk abroad, to contemplate nature quietly, and so take hold again of life. Leaning on a stick he bent his steps toward the city gate.

The nearest one, called *Porta Nuova*, is the very one which opens upon the finest scenery. Immediately on passing through it you find yourself in the open country; a fold of the hill hides the city and cuts off every sound that might come from it. Before you lies the winding road to Foligno; at the left the imposing mass of Mount Subasio; at the right the Umbrian plain with its farms, its villages, its cloudlike hills, on whose slopes pines, cedars, oaks, the vine, and the olive-tree shed abroad an incomparable brightness and animation. The whole country sparkles with beauty.

Assisi is approximately 0.7 miles in length and half as wide, with the Basilica di San Francesco at the northwest end and the road to Foligno and Spoleto at the southeast. The medieval castle, Rocca Maggiore, stands on the north center edge, and the city gate of Porta Nuova at the southeastern.

Francis had hoped by this sight to recover the delicious sensations of his youth. With the sharpened sensibility of the convalescent he breathed in the odors of the springtime, but springtime did not come to his heart, as he had expected. Nature had for him only a message of sadness. He had believed that the breezes of this beloved countryside would carry away the last shudders of the fever, and instead he felt in his heart a discouragement a thousandfold more painful than any physical illness. The miserable emptiness of his life suddenly appeared before him; he was terrified at his solitude, the solitude of a great soul in which there is no altar.

Memories of the past assailed him with intolerable bitterness. Seized with a disgust of himself, he found that his former ambitions seemed to him ridiculous or despicable. Francis went home overwhelmed with the weight of a new suffering.

In such hours of moral anguish we seek a refuge either in love or in faith. By a holy violence he was to arrive at last at a pure and virile faith, but the road to this point was long and sown thick with obstacles, and at the moment at which we have arrived he had not yet entered upon it; he did not even suspect its existence. All he knew was that pleasure leads to nothingness, to satiety and self-contempt.

He knew this, and yet he was about to throw himself once more into a life of pleasure. The body is so weak, so prone to return to the old paths, that it seeks them of itself the moment an energetic will does not stop it. Though no longer under any illusion with respect to it, Francis returned to his former life. Was he trying to divert his mind, to forget that day of bitter thought? We might suppose so, seeing the ardor with which he threw himself into his new projects.

An opportunity offered itself for him to realize his dreams of glory. A knight of Assisi, perhaps one of those who had been in captivity with him at Perugia, was preparing to go to Apulia under orders from "the gentle count" of Brienne, who was in the

Apulia is the region of Italy that resembles an index finger pointing east into the Adriatic Sea. During Francis's time, thousands of Crusaders visited Apulia and its many abbeys, churches, and relics before setting sail for the Holy Land from its coastal villages.

A recent biographer explains more about Walter of Brienne: "He had rescued Queen Sibila of Sicily from her imprisonment by the Germans in Alsace. With the King of France's blessing he had then sworn to recover her kingdom, which included Apulia on the mainland, and married her daughter. In approval of the enterprise Innocent III had created Walter Count of Lecce and Prince of Taranto. It was precisely the kind of career that Francis dreamed of for himself" (HOUSE, p. 45).

Innocent III was one of the most powerful of the medieval popes. Elected at the young age of 37, he ruled from 1198 to 1216.

south of Italy fighting on the side of Innocent III. Walter's renown was immense all through the Peninsula; he was held to be one of the most gallant knights of the time. Francis's heart bounded with joy; it seemed to him that at the side of such a hero he would soon cover himself with glory. His departure was decided upon, and he gave himself up, without reserve, to his joy.

He made his preparations with ostentatious prodigality. His equipment, of a princely luxury, soon became the universal subject of conversation. It was all the more talked about because the chief of the expedition, ruined perhaps by the revolution of 1202 or by the expenses of a long captivity, was constrained to order things much more modestly. Francis's companions were doubtless not slow to feel chafed by his ways and to promise themselves to make him cruelly expiate them. As for him, he perceived nothing of the jealousies that he was exciting, and night and day thought only of his future glory.

The day of departure arrived at last. Francis on horseback, the little buckler of a page on his arm, bade adieu to his natal city with joy, and with the little troop took the road to Spoleto which winds around the base of Mount Subasio.

What happened next? The documents do not say. They confine themselves to reporting that that very evening Francis had a vision, after which he decided to return to Assisi. It might not be far from the truth to conjecture that once on the way the young nobles took their revenge on the son of Bernardone for his princely airs. At twenty years old one hardly pardons things such as these.

Arriving at Spoleto, Francis took to his bed. A fever was consuming him; in a few hours he had seen all his dreams crumble away. The very next day he took the road back to Assisi.

So unexpected a return made a great stir in the little city, and was a cruel blow to his parents. As for

There were five primary types of travelers at this time in Europe: knights and royal communicants, religious men and women visiting other towns and provinces, sincere pilgrims, merchants, and a growing number of mischievous wanderers. Francis's enthusiasm might have been somewhat of the latter sort, which was increasingly of trouble for the late medieval Church. "By the beginning of the thirteenth century repeated canons directed against impostors, wandering scholars, and other ribalds . . . showed that restlessness had become the curse of Christendom" (WHICHER, p. 221).

Francis, he doubled his charities to the poor and sought to keep aloof from society, but the old companions came flocking about him from all quarters, hoping to find in him once more the tireless purveyor of their idle wants. He let them have their way.

Nevertheless a great change had taken place in Francis. Neither pleasures or work could hold his attention for long. He spent a portion of his days in long country rambles, often accompanied by a friend very different from the ones he had known up until now. The name of this friend is not known, but some indications suggest that it may have been Bombarone da Beviglia, the future Brother Elias.

In 1221, after their return from Syria, Francis appointed Brother Elias vicar of the Franciscan Order. Elias was present at Francis's death five years later, in October 1226, and it was Elias who, in large part, championed the speedy canonization of Francis and was responsible for the building of the basilica to house the body of the saint. Controversy surrounded Elias's leadership of the Order. (See MOORMAN, *chap. 10.)*

Francis now went back to reflecting as at the time of his recovery, but with less bitterness. His own heart and his friend agreed that it is not possible to trust either in pleasure or in glory and yet still find worthy causes to which to consecrate one's life. It is at this moment that religious thought seems to have awakened in him. From the moment that Francis saw this new way of life his desire to run in it had all the fiery impetuosity that he put into all his actions.

He was continually calling upon his friend and leading him apart into the most sequestered paths. Often Francis directed his steps to a grotto in the country near Assisi, which he entered alone. This rocky cave concealed in the midst of the olive trees became for faithful Franciscans that which Gethsemane is for all Christians. Here Francis relieved his overcharged heart by heavy groans. Sometimes, seized with a real horror for the disorders of his youth, he would implore mercy, but most of the time his face was turned toward the future. Feverishly Francis sought for that higher truth to which he longed to dedicate himself, that pearl of great price of which the Gospel speaks: "For everyone who asks receives, and everyone who searches finds, and for everyone who knocks, the door will be opened" (Mt. 7:8).

When he came out after long hours of seclusion, the pallor of his countenance and the painful tension of his features told plainly enough of the intensity of his asking and the violence of his knocks. The "inward man," to borrow the language of the mystics, was not yet formed in Francis, but it needed only the occasion to bring about the final break with the past. The occasion soon presented itself.

His friends were continually making efforts to induce him to take up old habits again. One day he invited them all to a sumptuous banquet. They thought they had conquered, and as in old times they proclaimed him king of the revels. The feast was prolonged far into the night and at its close the guests rushed out into the streets, which they filled with song and uproar. Suddenly they saw that Francis was no longer with them. After long searching, at last they discovered him far behind them, still holding in his hand his sceptre of king of misrule, but plunged in so profound a reverie that he seemed to be riveted to the ground and unconscious of all that was going on.

"What is the matter with you?" they cried, bustling about him as if to awaken him.

"Don't you see that he is thinking of taking a wife?" said one.

"Yes," answered Francis, arousing himself and looking at them with a smile that they did not recognize. "I am thinking of taking a wife more beautiful, more rich, more pure than you could ever imagine."

This reply marks a decisive stage in his inner life. By it he cut the last links that bound him to trivial pleasures. It remains for us to see through what struggles he was to give himself to God, after having torn himself free from the world. His friends probably understood nothing of all that had taken place, but he had become aware of the abyss that was opening between them and him. They soon accepted the situation.

No longer having any reason for caution, Francis gave up more than

One contemporary spiritual writer portrays the almost-converted Francis this way: "He had not yet attained to that inwardness of spirit that would enable him to make a fundamental decision about himself: that he had no choice but to lead the life of a homeless ascetic, a celestial wanderer. What lay ahead for him was not the cloistered life of a monk, or the privileged preserve of a bishop, but that of a perpetual outsider" (COWAN, p. 37).

ever to a passion for solitude. If he often wept over his past dissipations and wondered how he could have lived so long without tasting the bitterness of the dregs of the enchanted cup, he never allowed himself to be overwhelmed with vain regrets.

The poor had remained faithful to him. They gave him an admiration that he knew himself to be unworthy of, but that nevertheless had an infinite sweetness. The future grew bright to him in the light of their gratitude, of the timid, trembling affection that they dared not utter but that his heart revealed to him. Francis promised himself to do all he could to deserve it.

To understand these feelings one must understand the condition of the poor in a place such as Assisi. In an agricultural country poverty does not, as elsewhere, almost inevitably involve moral destitution, that degeneration of the entire human being that renders charity so difficult. Most of the poor people whom Francis knew were in straits because of war, of bad harvests, or of illness. In such cases material succor is but a small part. Sympathy is the thing needed above all. Francis had treasures of it to lavish on them.

As yet no influence strictly ecclesiastic had been felt by Francis. Doubtless there was in his heart the leaven of Christian faith that enters one's being without awareness, but the interior transformation that was going on in him was as yet the fruit of his own intuition. But this period was drawing to a close.

Francis was becoming calm by degrees, finding in the contemplation of nature joys that up to this time he had sipped only hastily, almost unconsciously, and of which he was now learning to relish the flavor. He drew from them not just soothingly; in his heart he felt

"…the interior transformation that was going on in him was as yet the fruit of his own intuition": A curious phrase from Sabatier, who appears to suggest that this was a period of time when Francis was preparing to be a mystic prior to his thorough "conversion." Bonaventure—who was prone to see God's deliberate hand in every event—says it this way: "Throughout all the time of which we have thus spoken, this great servant of God had neither master nor teacher to guide or instruct him, save only Christ our Lord, who, in addition to the gifts already bestowed upon him, was pleased now to visit him with the sweet consolations of His divine grace." For both Sabatier and Bonaventure, these actions of Francis were a prologue to a greater and more complete conversion soon to come.

new compassions springing to life, and with these the desire to act, to give himself, to cry aloud to these cities perched upon the hilltops, threatening as warriors who eye one another before the fray, that they should be reconciled and love one another.

Certainly, at this time Francis had no glimpse of what he was to become; but these hours are perhaps the most important in the evolution of his thought; it is to them that his life owes that air of liberty, that perfume of the fields that make it as different from the piety of the sacristy as from that of the drawing room.

The Umbrian region of Italy features many cities—like Assisi, Spoleto, Montefalco, and Gubbio—built on hilltops. It can be difficult to travel by train in Umbria, as the stations are often located in the valleys, sometimes two or three miles from the historic center of town; those walks, on hot summer afternoons, are not for the faint of heart.

About this time Francis made a pilgrimage to Rome, whether to ask the counsel of friends, as a penance imposed by a confession, or from a mere impulse, no one knows. Perhaps he thought that in a visit to the Holy Apostles, as people said then, he should find the answers to all the questions that he was asking himself.

This journey was marked by an important incident. Many a time when succoring the poor he had asked himself if he himself would be able to endure poverty. No one knows the weight of a burden until he has carried it, at least for a moment, upon his own shoulders. He desired to know what it is like to have nothing and to depend for bread upon the charity or the caprice of the passerby.

"...a visit to the Holy Apostles": The relics of the Apostles Peter and Paul are held, respectively, in the tombs of the Vatican and the Ostian Way, in the southernmost part of Rome. Even today, Rome is often referred to as "the city of the Apostles Peter and Paul." Visitors to the city today must see the historic Church of Santa Maria del Popolo where hang two great paintings of Caravaggio side-by-side: The Crucifixion of St. Peter and The Fall of Saul (1601–02).

There were swarms of beggars crowding the Piazza before the great basilica. He borrowed the rags of one of them, lending him his garment in exchange, and a whole day he stood there, fasting, with outstretched hand. The act was a great victory, the triumph of compassion over natural pride. Returning to Assisi, he doubled his kindnesses to those of whom he had truly the right to call himself the brother. With such sentiments he could not long escape the influence of the Church.

On all the roadsides in the environs of the city there were then, as now, numerous chapels. Very often Francis must have heard mass in these rustic sanctuaries, alone with the celebrant. Recognizing the tendency of simple natures to bring home to themselves everything that they hear, it is easy to understand his emotion and agitation when the priest, turning toward him, would read the Gospel for the day. The Christian ideal was revealed to him, bringing an answer to his secret anxieties. And when, a few moments later, he would plunge into the forest, all his thoughts would be with the poor carpenter of Nazareth, who placed himself in his path, saying, "Follow me."

"... the Piazza": The plaza surrounding St. Peter's Basilica in Rome.

Nearly two years had passed since the day that he felt the first shock, the first wave of his conversion. A life of renunciation now appeared to Francis as the goal of his efforts, but he felt that his spiritual novitiate was not yet ended. He suddenly experienced a bitter assurance of that fact.

He was riding on horseback one day, his mind more than ever possessed with the desire to lead a life of absolute devotion, when at a turn of the road he found himself face to face with a leper. The frightful malady had always inspired in him an invincible repulsion. He could not control a movement of horror, and by instinct he turned his horse in another direction.

But if the shock had been severe, the defeat was complete. Francis reproached himself bitterly; retracing his steps and springing from his horse he gave to the astounded sufferer all the money that he had, then kissed his hand as he would have done to a priest. This new victory marked a new era in his spiritual life.

It is far indeed from hatred of evil to love of good. They are more numerous than we think who, after some severe experience, have renounced what the ancient liturgies call "the world," with its pomps and lusts. But the greater number of those who have renounced the world have not at the bottom of their hearts the smallest grain of pure love. In vulgar souls disillusion leaves only a frightful egoism.

Francis was certainly not alone in his revulsion toward lepers. The medieval response to the disease was inherited from ancient days going back to the biblical book of Leviticus, chapter 13. In Francis's time, local priests performed a ceremony in which the priest would recite: "I forbid you to enter church, monastery, fair, mill, marketplace or tavern. . . . I forbid you ever to leave your house without your leper's costume . . . to live with any woman other than your own . . . to touch a well, or well cord, without your gloves . . . to touch children, or to give them anything . . . to eat or drink, except with lepers" (DAVIES, pp. 279–80).

CHAPTER THREE
The Church About 1209—Part One

St. Francis was inspired as much as any person may be, but it would be a palpable error to study him apart from his age and from the conditions in which he lived. We know that he desired and believed his life to be an imitation of Jesus, but what we know about the Christ is in fact so little, that St. Francis's life loses none of its strangeness for that. His conviction that he was but an imitator preserved him from all temptation to pride, and enabled him to proclaim his views with incomparable vigor without seeming in the least to be preaching himself.

We must therefore not isolate Francis from external influences or show him too dependent on them. During the period of his life at which we have now arrived, 1205–1206, the religious situation of Italy must more than at any other time have influenced his thought and urged him into the path that he finally entered.

The morals of the clergy were as corrupt as ever, rendering any serious reform impossible. If some among the heresies of the time were pure and without reproach, many were trivial and impure. Here and there a few voices were raised in protest, but the prophecies of Joachim of Fiore had no more power than those of St. Hildegard to put a stop to wickedness. The *little poor man*, driven away, cast out of doors by the creatures of Innocent III, saved Christianity.

We cannot here make a thorough study of the state of the Church at the beginning of the thirteenth century; it will suffice to trace some of its most prominent features.

The first glance at the secular clergy brings into startling prominence the ravages of simony; the traffic in ecclesiastical places was carried on with boundless audacity, and benefices were put up to the highest bidder. The bishops, for their part, found a thousand

> Sabatier does not exaggerate about the abuses in the Church of the twelfth and thirteenth centuries. The secular clergy were a frequent object of reformist derision. St. Anthony of Padua wrote around the time of Francis's death that they "flay the faithful by forced offerings, whereon they fatten their horses, their foals, and the sons of their concubines" (COULTON 2, p. 428).

methods, often most out of keeping with their calling, for extorting money from the simple priests. Violent, quarrelsome, contentious, they were held up to ridicule in popular ballads from one end of Europe to the other. As to the priests, they bent all their powers to accumulate benefices and secure inheritances from the dying, stooping to the most despicable measures for providing for their bastards.

The monastic orders were hardly more reputable. A great number of these had sprung up in the eleventh and twelfth centuries; their reputation for sanctity soon stimulated the liberality of the faithful, and thus fatally brought about their own decadence.

The clergy, though no longer respected, still overawed the people through the superstitious terror of their power. Here and there might have been perceived many a forewarning of direful revolts. The roads to Rome were crowded with monks hastening to claim the protection of the Holy See against the people among whom they lived. The pope would promptly declare an interdict, but it was not to be expected that such a resource would avail forever.

Yet we must not assume that all was corrupt in the bosom of the Church. Then, as always, the evil made more noise than the good, and the voices of those who desired a reformation aroused only passing interest.

At this time, in late medieval Europe, there were thousands of disenchanted youth, and others, who were in many cases university trained, traveling as vagabonds from city to city, writing lewd, humorous, and satirical verses in Latin in reaction to the Church and societal norms. These poets were generally called goliards, referring either to Goliath, the biblical giant slain by David, or to gula, the sin of gluttony. The movement was pervasive enough that St. Bernard of Clairvaux once referred to both Abelard, the controversial young theologian, and Arnold of Brescia (mentioned by Sabatier, below), both accused of heresy, as goliards. (See WHICHER.)

Jacques of Vitry, a thirteenth-century cardinal of the Church, tells an incredible story of a priest who was tired of the miserly habits of one of his flock who attended services each year only on Easter. The priest placed an old penny into the miser's mouth at communion, rather than a host. When the man asked about it afterwards, the priest persuaded him that God had changed the Eucharist into a penny as punishment for the man's lack of generosity. (See COULTON 2, p. 30.)

Among the populace there was superstition unimaginable. The pulpit, which ought to have shed abroad some little light, was as yet open only to the bishops, and the few pastors who did not neglect their duty in this regard accomplished very little, being too much absorbed in other duties. It was the birth of the mendicant orders that obliged the entire body of secular clergy to take up the practice of preaching.

"mendicant orders": Mendicant literally means "a beggar." Three mendicant orders were founded as reform movements in the thirteenth century—Franciscans, Dominicans, and Carmelites—emphasizing a vow to personal poverty and begging alms.

"secular clergy": Those who are ordained but do not follow a religious rule (as monks do). They are similar to what today we most often refer to as parish priests, as opposed to members of religious orders.

Public worship, reduced to liturgical ceremonies, no longer preserved anything that appealed to the intelligence; it was more and more becoming a sort of self-acting magic formula. Once upon this road, the absurd was not far distant. Those who deemed themselves pious told of miracles performed by relics with no need of aid from the moral act of faith.

In one case a parrot, being carried away by a kite, uttered the invocation dear to his mistress, "*Sancte Thoma adiuva me,*" (St. Thomas, help me!) and was miraculously rescued. In another, a merchant of Groningen, having purloined an arm of St. John the Baptist, grew rich as if by enchantment so long as he kept it concealed in his house, but was reduced to begging as soon as, his secret being discovered, the relic was taken away from him and placed in a church.

These stories, we must observe, do not come from ignorant enthusiasts, hidden away in obscure country places; they are given us by one of the most learned monks of his time, who relates them to a novice by way of forming his mind!

"tohu-bohu": This odd anachronism is used to mean something similar to the Genesis account of the early Creation as "formless and void"—chaotic, confused.

The list of the heresies of the thirteenth century is already long, but it is increasing every day, to the great joy of those erudite ones who are making strenuous efforts to classify everything in that tohu-bohu of mysticism and folly.

In that day heresy was very much alive; it was consequently very complex and its powers of transformation infinite. In certain counties of England there are at the present day villages having as many as eight and ten places of worship for only a few hundred inhabitants. Many of these people change their denomination every three or four years, returning to one and then leaving it again, and so on, as long as they live. Their leaders set the example, throwing themselves enthusiastically into each new movement only to leave it before long. They would all find it difficult to give an intelligible reason for these changes. They say that the Spirit guides them, and it would be unfair to disbelieve them, but the historian who should investigate conditions like these would lose his head in the labyrinth unless he made a separate study of each of these Protean movements.

A great part of Christendom was in a somewhat similar condition under Innocent III. But while the sects of which I have just spoken move in a very narrow circle of dogmas and ideas, in the thirteenth century every sort of excess followed in rapid succession. Still, a few general characteristics may be observed.

In the first place, heresies were no longer metaphysical subtleties as in earlier days; Arius and Priscillian, Nestorius and Eutyches were dead indeed. In the second place, they no longer arose in the upper and governing class, but proceeded especially from the inferior clergy and the common people. The blows that actually threatened the Church of the Middle Ages were struck by obscure laboring men, by the poor and the oppressed, who in their wretchedness

Sabatier refers to four leaders of early heretical movements.

"Arius" (256–336): A priest from Alexandria, Egypt, he argued that Christ, the Son of God, was not co-eternal with God, the Father.

"Priscillian": A Spaniard who taught extreme asceticism based on his belief in the basic evil of all matter. He was burned at the stake for suspicion of witchcraft in Avila, 383.

"Nestorius" (c. 381–451): A Patriarch of Constantinople, he argued that Jesus Christ had two distinct natures, human and divine, which were voluntarily, not truly, united.

"Eutyches": The leader, or Archimandrite, of a large monastery near Constantiople, he was sent into exile after the Council of Chalcedon (451), at the age of seventy-three, for teaching that Christ possessed only one nature, not two, after the Incarnation.

"Humiliati": *This odd group was an association of lay people who dressed plainly and practiced asceticism of various kinds, devoting themselves to charity. The Humiliati originated in Lombardy in the eleventh or early twelfth century. First approved by Innocent III in 1201, the Order witnessed the supression of its male branch in 1571 by a papal bull after one of its leaders attempted to murder an emissary of Pope Pius V who was charged with reforming it. There are still today some spiritual descendants of the Humiliati in Italy.*

"Arnold of Brescia": *A fascinating Italian monk who was active as a reformer before Francis's birth (d. 1155). Told to confine himself to a monastery, he refused and spoke out against abuses in the Church of his day. He preached about the sanctity of poverty and even challenged the exclusive right of priests to administer the sacraments and hear confessions. Eventually, Arnold was hanged by the Roman authorities, with the blessing of the Church, and his ashes were scattered over the Tiber River so that his followers would not venerate his bones.*

"Waldensians": *A reform movement from the twelfth and thirteenth centuries founded by Peter Waldo from the city of Lyons. The Waldensians, also called "the poor of Lyons," claimed to represent a true remnant who, from within, had been resisting the Catholic Church and attempting to reform it since the days of Constantine in the fourth century.*

and degradation felt that she had failed in her mission. No sooner was a voice uplifted, preaching austerity and simplicity, than it drew together not only the laity, but members of the clergy as well.

Two great currents are apparent: on one side the Cathars, on the other, innumerable sects revolting from the Church by their very fidelity to Christianity and the desire to return to the primitive Church. Among the sects of the second category the close of the twelfth century saw in Italy the rise of the Poor Men, who without doubt were a part of the movement of Arnold of Brescia. They denied the efficacy of sacraments administered by unworthy hands. A true attempt at reform was made by the Waldensians. Their history, although better known, still remains obscure on certain sides. Their name, Poor Men of Lyons, recalls the former movement, with which they were in close agreement, as also with the Humiliati. All these names involuntarily suggest that by which St. Francis afterward called his Order.

The analogy between the inspiration of Peter Waldo, founder of the Waldensians, and that of St. Francis was so close that one might be tempted to believe the latter a sort of imitation of the former. But this would be a mistake: The same causes produced in all quarters the same effects; ideas of reform, of a return to Gospel poverty, were in the air, and this helps us to understand how it was that before many years the Franciscan preaching reverberated through the entire world. If at the outset the careers of these two men were alike, their later lives were very different. Waldo, driven into heresy almost in spite of himself, was obliged to accept the consequences of the premises that he himself had laid down, while Francis, remaining the obedient son of the Church, bent all his efforts to develop the inner life in himself and his disciples. It is indeed most likely that through his father Francis had become acquainted with the movement of the Poor of Lyons. Hence his oft-repeated counsels to his friars of the duty of submission to the clergy. When he went to seek the approbation of Innocent III, it is evident that the prelates with whom he had relations warned him, by the very example of Waldo, of the dangers inherent in his own movement.

Waldo had gone to Rome in 1179, accompanied by a few followers, to ask at the same time the approbation of their translation of the Scriptures into the venacular and the permission to preach. They were granted both requests on condition of gaining for their preaching the authorization of their local clergy. Walter Map (d. 1210), who was charged with their examination, was constrained, while ridiculing their simplicity, to admire their poverty and zeal for the apostolic life.

> *"... while Francis, remaining the obedient son of the Church": It is important to realize that heresy is primarily a charge of insolence and disobedience, more so than a misinterpretation of doctrine. It is a question of challenging established order and authority.*

Two or three years later they met a very different reception at Rome, and in 1184 they were anathematized by the Council of Verona. From that day nothing could stop them, even to the forming of a new Church. They multiplied with a rapidity hardly exceeded afterward by the Franciscans. By the end of the twelfth century we find them spread abroad from Hungary to Spain; the first attempts to hunt them down were made in the latter country. Other countries were at first satisfied with treating them as excommunicated persons.

Obliged to hide themselves, reduced to the impossibility of holding their chapters, which ought to have come together once or twice a year, and which, had they done so, might have maintained among them a certain unity of doctrine, the Waldensians rapidly underwent a change according to their environment. Some obstinately insisted upon calling themselves good Catholics; others went so far as to preach the overthrow of the hierarchy and the uselessness of sacraments. The multiplicity of differing and even hostile branches seemed to develop almost hourly. Under pretext of pilgrimages to Rome they were always on the road. The methods of travel of that day were peculiarly favorable to the diffusion of ideas. While retailing news to those whose hospitality they received, they would speak of the unhappy state of the Church and the reforms that were needed.

As a young child, St. Bonaventure was healed through Francis, and later became one of the first to record his legend. After Bonaventure's Life was written and distributed, the Chapter of Paris (1266), an official gathering of Franciscan leaders, ordered that all previous biographies of Francis be destroyed. The earlier lives of Francis written by Thomas of Celano were preserved only in certain Cistercian and Benedictine monastery libraries.

It was Bonaventure's life of Francis that inspired the great painter Giotto with the subject matter for twenty-eight fresco paintings depicting popular scenes from Francis's life. They can still be seen in the upper church of the Basilica di San Francesco in Assisi.

CHAPTER FOUR

The Church About 1209—Part Two

The most powerful and determined enemies of the Church were the Cathars. Sincere, audacious, often learned and keen in argument, having among them some choice spirits and people of great intellectual powers, they were the preeminent heretics of the thirteenth century. Their revolt did not bear upon points of detail and questions of discipline, like that of the early Waldensians; it had a definite doctrinal basis, taking issue with the whole body of Catholic dogma. But, although this heresy flourished in Italy and under the very eyes of St. Francis, there is need to discuss it only briefly. His work may have received many infiltrations from the Waldensian movement, but Catharism was wholly foreign to it.

This is naturally explained by the fact that St. Francis never consented to occupy himself with questions of doctrine. For him faith was not of the intellectual but the moral domain; it is the consecration of the heart. Time spent in dogmatizing appeared to him as time lost. The Cathars, then, had no direct influence upon St. Francis.

Catharist doctrine rested upon the antagonism of two principles, one bad, the other good. The first had created matter; the second, the soul, which, for generation after generation passes from one body to another until it achieves salvation. Matter is the cause and the seat of evil. All contact with it constitutes a blemish; consequently the Cathars renounced marriage and property and advocated suicide. All this was mixed up with the most complicated cosmological myths.

Perhaps the most telling example of the radical Catharist distinction between matter and spirit was in their depiction of the meaning of the cross of Christ. The Cathar cross, often depicted on tombstones in the regions of Languedoc and in the lands of the former Yugoslavia, is a thorough triumph of spirit over matter. An upright and serene Jesus is luminously shown to be as a tree of life, reaching toward heaven, moon, stars, or sunburst—the Land of Light—a triumph over the world of twisted, dark matter.

This dualism of the Cathars stood in stark contrast to Francis's joyful hymn, "The Canticle of the Sun" (also known as "The Canticle of the Creatures"), in which he praises creation in each of the four basic elements from antiquity: water, air, fire, earth. (See chap. 20.)

With all his energy Innocent III had not been able to check this evil in the states of the Church. The case of Viterbo tells much of the difficulty of repressing it. In March 1199, the pope wrote to the clergy and people of this town to recall to their minds, and at the same time to increase, the penalties pronounced against heresy. For all that, the Patarini (as the Cathars were called in Italy) had the majority in 1205, and succeeded in naming one of themselves consul.

The wrath of the pontiff at this event was unbounded. He fulminated a bull menacing the city with fire and sword, and commanding the neighboring towns to throw themselves upon her if within a fortnight she had not given satisfaction. It was all in vain: the Patarini were dealt with only as a matter of form; it needed the presence of the pope himself to assure the execution of his orders and obtain the demolition of the houses of the heretics and their abettors (autumn of 1207).

Italy may well be grateful to St. Francis. He did not pause to demonstrate by syllogisms or theological theses the vanity of the Catharist doctrines; but he made a new ideal to shine out before the eyes of his contemporaries, an ideal before which all these fantastic sects vanished as birds of the night take flight at the first rays of the sun. A great part of St. Francis's power came to him thus through his systematic avoidance of polemics. The latter is always more or less a form of spiritual pride. It only deepens the chasm that it undertakes to fill up. Truth needs not to be proved; it is its own witness.

The only weapon that he would use against the wicked was the holiness of a life so full of love as to enlighten and revive those

"the Patarini": Sabatier explains in a footnote: *"The most current name in Italy [for the Cathars] was that of the Patarini, given them no doubt from their inhabiting the quarter of second-hand dealers in Milan: la contrada dei Patari, found in many cities. Patari! is still the cry of the ragpickers in the small towns of Provence. In the thirteenth century Patarino and Catharo were synonyms."* One of Sabatier's contemporaries explains further: *"In the sordid alleys of Milan, to which the degraded trades were consigned as to a ghetto, the booths of the sellers of old iron and rags, the bazaar of the Pataria, there thus sprang up an enthusiastic Christianity"* (GEBHART, p. 55). Rags were raw material for making paper at this time. For whatever reason, this trade was common among the members of the Cathars.

about him, and compel them to love. The disappearance of Catharism in Italy, without an upheaval, and above all without the Inquisition, is thus an indirect result of the Franciscan movement, and not the least important among them. At the voice of the Umbrian reformer Italy roused herself, recovered her good sense and fine temper. She cast out those doctrines of pessimism and death, as a robust organism casts out morbid substances.

But Francis was not immune to the influence of all heresy. As we discussed above, Francis's thought ripened in an atmosphere thoroughly saturated with the ideas of the Poor Men of Lyons. Unconsciously to himself they entered into his being. Similarly, the prophecies of one Calabrian abbot exerted upon St. Francis an influence more difficult to appreciate, but no less profound.

Standing on the confines of Italy and as it were at the threshold of Greece, Joachim of Fiore was the last link in a chain of monastic prophets who during nearly four hundred years succeeded one another in the monasteries and hermitages of southern Italy. The most famous among them had been St. Nilo, a sort of untamed John the Baptist living in desert places but suddenly emerging from them when his duties of maintaining the right called him elsewhere. We see him on one occasion appearing in Rome itself, to announce to pope and emperor the unloosing of the divine wrath.

Sabatier explains in a footnote: "I do not assert that no trace of Catharism is to be found after the ministry of St. Francis, but it was no longer a force, and no longer endangered the very existence of the Church."

The direct influence of Francis was actually only one part of the struggle against the Cathars, who were prevalent in southern France and central and northern Italy at this time. Innocent III declared the fight against the Cathar heresy to be a true crusade in 1209, equivalent to the crusades to retake the Holy Land. St. Dominic founded the Dominican Order just a few years after the birth of the Franciscans in response to the growth of the Cathars. The Inquisition followed soon thereafter.

"St. Nilo, a sort of untamed John the Baptist": Nilus of Calabria (c. 910–1005), of Greek descent, inspired by Athanasius's Life of St. Anthony, was remarkable for two things: his attempts to reform corruptions in Western monasteries through asceticism, and his unsuccessful efforts to reconcile Eastern (Byzantine) and Western (Benedictine) monasticism.

Scattered in the Alpine solitudes of the Basilicata region in southern Italy, these Calabrian hermits were continually obliged to retreat higher and higher into the mountains to escape the populace, who, pursued by pirates, were taking refuge there. They thus passed their lives between heaven and earth, with two seas for their horizon. Disquieted by fear of the corsairs and by the war-cries whose echoes reached even to them, they turned their thoughts toward the future. The ages of great terror are also the ages of great hope; it is to the captivity of Babylon that we owe, with the second part of Isaiah, the pictures of the future that have not yet ceased to charm the soul of humanity; Nero's persecutions gave us the Apocalypse of St. John, and the paroxysms of the twelfth century the eternal gospel.

Converted after a life of dissipation, Joachim of Fiore traveled extensively in the Holy Land, Greece, and Constantinople. Returning to Italy he began, though a layman, to preach in the out-skirts of Rende and Cosenza. Later on he joined the Cistercians of Cortale, near Catanzaro, and there took vows. Shortly after being elected abbot of the monastery in spite of refusal and even flight, he was seized after a few years with the nostalgia of solitude, and sought from Pope Lucius III a discharge from his functions (1181), that he might consecrate all his time to the works that he had in mind. The pope granted his request and even permitted him to go wherever he might deem best in the interest of his work. Then began for Joachim a life of wandering from monastery to monastery that carried him even as far as Lombardy, to Verona, where we find him with Pope Urban III.

When he returned to the south, a group of disciples gathered around him to hear his explanations of the most obscure passages of the Bible. Whether he desired to or not he was obliged to receive them, to talk with them, to give them a Rule, and, finally, to install them in the very heart of the Sila, the Black Forest of Italy, over against the highest peak, in gorges where the silence is interrupted only by the murmurs of the Arno and the Neto, which have their source not far from there.

This new Athos received the name of Fiore (flower), trans-parent symbol of the hopes of its founder. It was there that he put the finishing touch to writings that, after fifty years of neglect, were

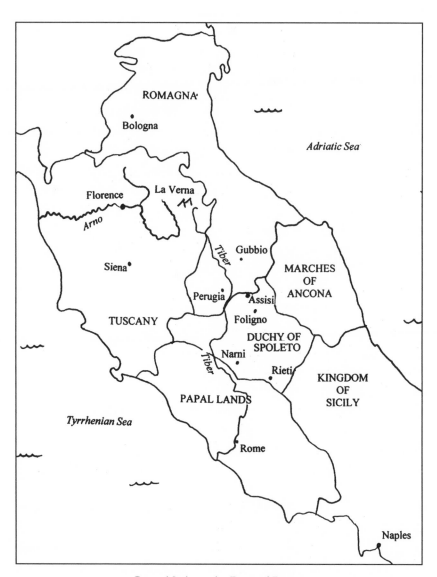

Central Italy in the Days of Francis

Joachim had a similar effect as that of Francis on his followers: "Joachim's one great interest was to study the prophecies; his one great pleasure to celebrate mass. During mass he was in a sort of ecstasy, his face (usually the colour of a dry leaf) became like that of an angel, and sometimes he wept. When he preached, the young monks gazed on his face as if he were an angel presiding over them, and when he knelt in prayer his countenance was aglow as if he looked upon Christ face to face" (SEDGWICK, vol. 1, p. 41).

Sabatier adds this note about "Sila, the Black Forest of Italy": "La Sila is a wooded mountain, situated eastward from Cosenza, which the peasants call Monte Nero. The summits are nearly 2,000 meters above the sea."

The allegorical method was a common and accepted method of biblical interpretation throughout the later Middle Ages. By this method, for instance, Meister Eckhart, a German Dominican mystic who lived a century after Francis, taught that the true meaning of Christmas was the mystical birth of God in human hearts. The allegorical method persists today, perhaps most commonly in interpretations of the Song of Songs as more than a beautiful story of human love; it is also an allegory of the intimacy possible in the Divine-human relationship.

to become the starting-point of all heresies, and the ailment of all souls burdened with the salvation of Christendom. The people of the first half of the thirteenth century, too much occupied with other things, did not perceive that the spiritual streams at which they were drinking descended from the snowy mountaintops of Calabria. It is always thus with mystical influences. There is in them something vague, tenuous, and penetrating that escapes an exact estimation.

He always remained riveted to the text, upon which he commented in the allegorical method, and by this method he brought out the most fantastic improbabilities. A few pages of his books would wear out the most patient reader, but in these fields, burnt over by theological arguments more drying than the winds of the desert, fields where one at first perceives only stones and thistles, one comes at last to the charming oasis, with repose and dreams in its shade.

The exegesis of Joachim of Fiore in fact led up to a sort of philosophy of history; its grand lines were calculated to make a striking appeal to the imagination. The life of humanity is divided into three periods: In the first, under the reign of the Father, humanity lived under the rigor of the law; in the second, reigned over by the Son, people live under the rule of grace; in the third, the Spirit will reign and humanity will live in the plenitude of love. The first is the period of servile obedience; the second, that of filial obedience; the third, that of liberty. In the first, people lived in fear; in the second, they rest in faith; in the third, they shall burn with love. The first saw the shining of the stars; the second sees the whitening of the dawn; the third will behold the glory of the day. The first produced nettles, the second gives roses, the third will be the age of lilies.

If now we consider that in the thought of Joachim the third period, the Age of the Spirit, was about to open, we will understand with what enthusiasm people hailed the words that restored joy to hearts still disturbed with millenarian fears.

It is evident that St. Francis knew these radiant hopes. Who knows even that it was not the Calabrian Seer who awoke his heart to its transports of love? If this be so, Joachim was not merely his precursor; he was his true spiritual father. However this may be, St. Francis found in Joachim's thought many of the elements that, unconsciously to himself, were to become the foundation of his institute.

The noble disdain that Francis shows for all people of learning, and that he sought to inculcate upon his Order, was for Joachim one of the characteristics of the new era. "The truth that remains hidden to the wise," he says, "is revealed to babes. Dialectics closes that which is open, obscures that which is clear; it is the mother of useless talk, of rivalries and blasphemy. Learning does not edify, and it may destroy, as is proved by the scribes of the Church, swollen with pride and arrogance, who by dint of reasoning fall into heresy."

This was the time when Europe's first great universities were first flourishing: in Bologna (Italy), Paris (France), and Oxford (England). Others soon sprouted throughout Europe, including Italy, even before Francis's death: Naples (1224), Padua (1222), Reggie, Siena, and others.

We have seen that the return to Gospel simplicity had become a necessity. All the heretical sects were on this point in accord with pious Catholics, but no one spoke in a manner so Franciscan as Joachim of Fiore. Not only did he make voluntary poverty one of the characteristics of the age of lilies, but he speaks of it in his pages with so profound, so living an emotion, that St. Francis could do little more than repeat his words. The ideal monk whom Joachim describes, whose only property is a lyre, is a true Franciscan before the letter, him of whom the *Poverello* of Assisi always dreamed.

The feeling of nature also bursts forth in him with incomparable vigor. One day he was preaching in a chapel that was plunged in almost total darkness, the sky being quite overcast with clouds. Suddenly the clouds broke away, the sun shone, and the church was flooded with light. Joachim paused, saluted the sun, intoned the *Veni Creator*, and led his congregation out to gaze upon the landscape.

It would be by no means surprising if toward 1205 Francis should have heard of this prophet, toward whom so many hearts were turning, this anchorite who, gazing up into heaven, spoke with Jesus as a friend talks with his friend, yet knew also how to come down to console people and warm the faces of the dying at his own breast.

Meanwhile, at the other end of Europe, in the heart of Germany, the same causes had produced the same effects. From the excess of the people's sufferings and the despair of religious souls was being born a movement of apocalyptic mysticism that seemed to have secret communication with the one that was rousing the Peninsula. They had the same views of the future, the same anxious expectation of new cataclysms, joined with a prospect of a reviving of the Church.

"Cry with a loud voice," said her guardian angel to St. Elizabeth of Schönau (d. 1164), "cry to all nations: Woe! for the whole world has become darkness. The Lord's vine has withered, there is no one to tend it. The Lord has sent laborers, but they have all been found idle. The head of the Church is ill and her members are dead. . . . Shepherds of my Church, you are sleeping, but I shall awaken you! Kings of the earth, the cry of your iniquity has risen even to me."

"Divine justice," said St. Hildegard (d. 1178), "shall have its hour. The last of the seven epochs symbolized by the seven days of creation has arrived, the judgments of God are about to be accomplished; the empire and the papacy, sunk into impiety, shall crumble away together. . . . But upon their ruins shall appear a new nation of

God, a nation of prophets illuminated from on high, living in poverty and solitude. Then the divine mysteries shall be revealed, and the saying of Joel shall be fulfilled; the Holy Spirit shall shed abroad upon the people the dew of his prophecies, of his wisdom and holiness."

These hopes were not wholly confounded. In the evening of his days the prophet of Fiore was able, like a new Simeon, to utter his *Nunc dimittis*, and for a few years Christendom could turn in amazement to Assisi as to a new Bethlehem.

————————— ◦◦◦ —————————

Dante, the great Florentine poet of The Divine Comedy, *expresses a commonly held view in the century after Francis's death: Joachim was "gifted with the prophetic spirit" (Paradiso, canto xii); he was a John the Baptist for the life, teaching, and reform brought by Francis.*

————————— ◦◦◦ —————————

CHAPTER FIVE

Struggles and Triumph
(Spring 1206–February 24, 1209)

Since his abrupt return from Spoleto, life in his father's house had daily become more difficult. Bernardone's self-love had received from his son's embarrassment such a wound as with common people is never healed. He might provide, without counting it, money to be swallowed up in dissipation so that his son might stand on an equal footing with the young nobles. But he could never resign himself to see him giving with lavish hands to every beggar in the streets.

Francis, continually plunged in reverie and spending his days in lonely wanderings in the fields, was no longer of the least use to his father. Months passed and the distance between the two men grew ever wider, and the gentle and loving Pica could do nothing to prevent a rupture that from this time appeared to be inevitable. Francis soon came to feel only one desire—to flee from the abode where, in the place of love, he found only reproaches, upbraidings, anguish.

The faithful confidant of his earlier struggles had been obliged to leave him, and this absolute solitude weighed heavily upon Francis's warm and loving heart. He did what he could to escape it, but no one understood him. The ideas that he was beginning timidly to express evoked from those to whom he spoke only mocking smiles or the head-shakings that people sure they are right bestow upon one who is marching straight to madness. He even went to open his mind to the bishop, but the latter understood no more than others his vague, incoherent plans, filled with ideas impossible to realize and possibly subversive.

Among the numerous chapels in the suburbs of Assisi there was one that he particularly loved, that of San Damiano. It was reached by a few minutes walk over a stony path, almost trackless, under olive trees, amid odors of lavender and rosemary. Standing on the top of a hillock, one can see the entire plain through a curtain of cypresses and pines that seem to be trying to hide the humble hermitage and set up an ideal barrier between it and the world.

Served by a poor priest who had scarcely the wherewithal for necessary food, the sanctuary was falling into ruin. There was nothing in the interior but a simple altar of masonry, and on a reredos one of those Byzantine crucifixes still so numerous in Italy, where through the work of the artists of the time has come down to us something of the terrors that agitated the twelfth century. In general, the Crucified One, frightfully lacerated, with bleeding wounds, appears to seek to inspire only grief and compunction; that of San Damiano, on the contrary, has an expression of inexpressible calm and gentleness. Instead of closing the eyelids in eternal surrender to the weight of suffering, it looks down in self-forgetfulness, and its pure, clear gaze says, not "I suffer," but, "Come unto me."

The crucifix of San Damiano, so important in the life of Francis, was taken to the Chapel of San Giorgio by the Sisters of St. Clare after Clare's death. They took it with them when they relocated to San Giorgio, leaving behind the more remote San Damiano. The eyes of the crucifix are specifically mentioned by Sabatier and the earlier biographers. This reminds us of a painter of icons who always leaves the eyes for last, as the eyes are the most important feature—the primary opening into the figure represented.

One day Francis was praying before the poor altar: "Great and glorious God, and you, Lord Jesus, I pray you, shed abroad your light in the darkness of my mind. . . . Be found in me, Lord, so that in all things I may act only in accordance with your holy will."

Thus he prayed in his heart, and behold, little by little it seemed to him that his gaze could not detach itself from that of Jesus. He felt something marvelous taking place in and around him. The sacred victim took on life, and in the outward silence he was aware of a voice that softly stole into the very depths of his heart, speaking to him an ineffable language. Jesus accepted his oblation. Jesus desired his labor, his life, all his being, and the heart of the poor solitary was already bathed in light and strength.

This vision marks the final triumph of Francis. His union with Christ was consummated. From this time he could exclaim with the mystics of every age, "My beloved is mine, and I am his." For the first time, no doubt, Francis had been brought into direct, personal, intimate contact with Jesus Christ.

This look of love cast upon the crucifix, this mysterious colloquy with the compassionate victim, was never to cease. At San Damiano, St. Francis's piety took on its outward appearance and its originality. From that time his way was plain before him. Coming out from the sanctuary, he gave the priest all the money he had about him to keep a lamp always burning, and with ravished heart he returned to Assisi. He had decided to leave his father's house and undertake the restoration of the chapel, after having broken the last ties that bound him to the past. A horse and a few pieces of brightly colored cloths were all that he possessed. Arriving at home he made a packet of the cloths, and mounting his horse he set out for Foligno. This city was then as now the most important commercial town of all the region. Its fairs attracted the whole population of Umbria and the Sabines. Bernardone had often taken his son there, and Francis speedily succeeded in selling all he had brought. He even parted with his horse, and full of joy set out upon the road to Assisi.

This act was to him most important; it marked his final rupture with the past. From this day on his life was to be in all points the opposite of what it had been. The Crucified had given himself to him; he on his side had given himself to the Crucified without reserve or return. To uncertainty, disquietude of soul, anguish, longing for an unknown good, bitter regrets, had succeeded a delicious calm, the ecstasy of the lost child who finds his mother and forgets in a moment the torture of his heart.

From Foligno he returned directly to San Damiano; it was not necessary to pass through the city, and he was in haste to put his projects

---

Historian G. G. Coulton is critical of Sabatier's account of this famous scene. Coulton refers to Francis's as a "pious theft." He writes: "It is very difficult to understand how, in the face of the early biographers, so admirable a writer as M. Sabatier can speak of the Foligno incident as though the horse and cloth had really been the Saint's own" (COULTON 2, p. 31).

This is the story of the prodigal son turned on its head! In the parable, the son wastes his inheritance in dissipation; Francis has taken the first decisive step toward renouncing his worldly goods. In both the parable and in Francis's life, the son leaves his father only to return to him, begging forgiveness and finding grace. The difference of course, in Francis's case, is that he was acting in obedience to his heavenly Father.

into execution. The poor priest was surprised enough when Francis handed over to him the whole product of his sale. He doubtless thought that a passing quarrel had occurred between Bernardone and his son, and for greater prudence refused the gift. But Francis so insisted upon remaining with him that he finally gave him leave to do so. As to the money, now become useless, Francis cast it as a worthless object upon a window-seat in the chapel.

Meanwhile Bernardone, disturbed by his son's failure to return, sought for him in all quarters, and was not long in learning of his presence at San Damiano. In a moment he perceived that Francis was lost to him. Resolved to try every means, he collected a few neighbors, and furious with rage hastened to the hermitage to snatch him away, if necessary, by force.

But Francis knew his father's violence. When he heard the shouts of those who were in pursuit of him he felt his courage fail and hurried to a hiding-place that he had prepared for himself for precisely such an emergency. Bernardone ransacked every corner, but was obliged at last to return to Assisi without his son. Francis remained hidden for long days, weeping and groaning, imploring God to show him the path he ought to follow. Notwithstanding his fears he had an infinite joy at heart, and at no price would he have turned back.

This seclusion could not last long. Francis perceived this and told himself that for a newly made knight of Christ he was cutting a very pitiful figure. Arming himself, therefore, with courage, he went one day to the city to present himself before his father and make known to him his resolution. It is easy to imagine the changes wrought in his appearance by these few weeks of seclusion, much of them passed in mental anguish. When he appeared, pale, cadaverous, his clothes in tatters, upon what is now the Piazza Nuova, where hundreds of children play all day long, he was greeted with a great shout, *"Pazzo, Pazzo!"* ("A madman! A madman!") *"Un pazzo ne fa cento"* ("One madman makes a hundred more"), says the proverb, but one must have seen the delirious excitement of the street children of Italy at the sight of a madman to gain an idea how true it is. The moment the magic cry resounds they rush into the street with frightful din, and while their parents look on from the windows, they surround the unhappy sufferer with wild dances mingled with songs, shouts, and savage howls. They throw stones at him, fling mud upon him, blindfold him; if he flies into a rage, they double their insults; if he weeps or begs for pity, they repeat his cries and mimic his sobs and supplications without respite and without mercy.

Bernardone soon heard the clamor that filled the narrow streets and went out to enjoy the show. Suddenly, he thought he heard his own name and that of his son, and bursting with shame and rage he perceived Francis. Throwing himself upon him, as if to throttle him, he dragged him into the house and cast him, half dead, into a dark closet. Everything was brought to bear to change the prisoner's resolve, but all in vain. At last, wearied out and desperate, Bernardone left him in peace, though not without having firmly bound him.

A few days later he was obliged to be absent for a short time. Pica, his wife, understood only too well his grievances against Francis, but feeling that violence would be of no avail she resolved to try gentleness. It was all in vain. Then, no longer able to see him tortured in this way, she set him free. Francis returned straight to San Damiano.

Bernardone, on his return, went so far as to strike Pica in punishment for her weakness. Then, unable to tolerate the thought of seeing his son the jest of the whole city, he tried to procure his expulsion from the territory of Assisi. Going to San Damiano he summoned him to leave the country. This time Francis did not try to hide. Boldly

Francis demonstrated a taste for holy foolishness throughout his life. No doubt his growing spiritual confidence took some measure of pleasure in being ridiculed by the townspeople as he returned to Assisi. Only a few years later, Francis and Brother Rufino preached in Assisi wearing only their underwear. According to another story, when Brother Bernard was sent by Francis to nearby Bologna, Bernard too was set upon by the children of that city. Bernard, probably as Francis had taught him, bore it all with visible joy and even made his way further—to the marketplace—so that the impact of his physical appearance of foolishness would be even greater. Adults joined the children in throwing dust and stones at him, pushing him, and plucking at the hood of his tattered tunic. The story tells that Bernard returned day after day to the marketplace for the same treatment. Finally, someone from the crowd asked him where his great patience and holiness arose from, and Bernard pulled out a copy of Francis's Rule. That is how, according to legend, Bologna and many other towns became the home of early Franciscans.

presenting himself, he declared that not only would nothing induce him to abandon his resolutions, but moreover, having become the servant of Christ, he had no longer to receive orders from his father. As Bernardone launched out into invective, reproaching him with the enormous sums that he had cost him, Francis showed him by a gesture the money that he had brought back from the sale at Foligno lying on the window-ledge. The father greedily seized it and went away, resolving to appeal to the magistrates. Bernardone could do no more than disinherit his son, or at least induce him of his own accord to renounce all claim upon his inheritance.

When called upon to appear before the episcopal tribunal Francis experienced a lively joy. His mystical espousals to the Crucified One were now to receive a sort of official consecration. To this Jesus, whom he had so often blasphemed and betrayed by word and conduct, he would now be able with equal publicity to promise obedience and fidelity.

It is easy to imagine the sensation that all this caused in a small town like Assisi, and the crowd that on the appointed day pressed toward the Piazza of Santa Maria Maggiore, where the bishop pronounced sentence. Everyone held Francis to be assuredly mad, but they anticipated with relish the shame and rage of Bernardone, whom everyone detested, and whose pride was so well punished by all of this.

The bishop first set forth the case, and advised Francis to simply give up all his property. To the great surprise of the crowd the latter, instead of replying, retired to a room in the bishop's palace, and immediately reappeared absolutely naked, holding in his hand the packet into which he had rolled his clothes; these he laid down before the bishop with the little money that he still had kept, saying, "Listen, all of you, and understand it well. Until this time I have called Peter Bernardone my father, but now I desire to serve God. This is why I return to him this money, for which he has given himself so much trouble, as well as my clothing, and all that I have had from him, for from henceforth I desire to say nothing else than 'Our Father, who art in heaven.'"

A long murmur arose from the crowd when Bernardone was seen to gather up and carry off the clothing without the least evidence of compassion, while the bishop was obliged to take under his mantle the poor Francis, who was trembling with emotion and cold.

The scene of the judgment hall made an immense impression. The ardor, simplicity, and indignation of Francis had been so profound and sincere that scoffers were disconcerted. On that day he won for himself a secret sympathy in many souls. The incident is simply a new manifestation of Francis's character, with its ingenuousness, its exaggerations, its longing to establish a complete harmony, a literal correspondence, between words and actions.

After emotions such as he had just experienced he felt the need of being alone, of realizing his joy, of singing the liberty he had finally achieved along all the lines where once he had so deeply suffered, so ardently struggled. Leaving the city by the nearest gate, he plunged into the deserted paths that climb the sides of Mount Subasio.

Other biographers recount that Francis was wearing one garment underneath his father's expensive clothes—significantly—"a hair shirt next to his skin" according to The Legend of the Three Companions, *representing an ascetic's devotion to God* (THREE, p. 80). *On the contrary, Giotto's famous fresco painting on the north wall of the upper church in the Basilica di San Francesco depicts a naked Francis under the bishop's robe. Either way, "Francis was a master of dramatic gestures and visual tableaux, and, unsurprisingly, representations of these played an important part in his cult"* (HOLMES, p. 55). *Chesterton adds, he "was one of the founders of the mediaeval drama"* (CHESTERTON, p. 78).

It was the early spring. Here and there were still great drifts of snow, but under the ardor of the March sun winter seemed to own itself vanquished. In the midst of this mysterious and bewildering harmony the heart of Francis felt a delicious thrill; all his being was calmed and uplifted; the soul of things caressed him gently and shed upon him peace. An unaccustomed happiness swept over him and he made the forest resound with his hymns of praise.

So Francis went on his way, deeply inhaling the odors of spring, singing at the top of his voice one of those songs of French chivalry that he had learned in days gone by. The forest in which he was walking was the usual retreat of such people of Assisi and its environs as had reason for hiding. Some ruffians, aroused by his voice, suddenly fell upon him. "Who are you?" they asked. "I am the herald of the great King," he answered, "but what is that to you?"

His only garment was an old mantle that the bishop's gardener had lent him at his master's request. They stripped it from him, and throwing him into a ditch full of snow they said, "There is your place, poor herald of God."

The robbers gone, he shook off the snow that covered him, and after many efforts succeeded in extricating himself from the ditch. Stiff with cold, with no other covering than a worn-out shirt, he none the less resumed his singing, happy to suffer and thus to accustom himself the better to understand the words of the Crucified One.

He directed his steps toward Gubbio, where he knew that he would find a friend. Perhaps this was he who had been his confidant on his return from Spoleto. Whoever it was, he received from him a tunic, and a

"He went out half-naked...a man without a father. He was penniless, he was parentless, he was to all appearances without a trade or a plan or a hope in the world; and as he went under the frosty trees, he burst suddenly into song" (CHESTERTON, p. 66).

few days later set out to return to his dear San Damiano. After having fashioned for himself a hermit's dress, he began to go into the squares and open places of the city. Having sung a few hymns there, he would announce to those who gathered around him his project of restoring the chapel.

Many deemed him mad, but others were deeply moved by the remembrance of the past. As for Francis, deaf to mockery, he spared himself no labor, carrying upon his shoulders, so ill-fitted for severe toil, the stones that were given him. During this time the poor priest of San Damiano felt his heart swelling with love for this companion who had at first caused him such embarrassment, and he strove to prepare for him his favorite dishes. Francis soon perceived it and his delicacy took alarm at the expense that he caused his friend. Thanking him, he resolved to beg his food from door to door.

It was not an easy task. Each hour, so to speak, brought to him a new struggle. One day he was going through the town begging for oil for the lamps of San Damiano, when he arrived at a house where a banquet was going on. A great number of his former companions were there, singing and dancing. At the sound of those well-known voices he felt as if he could not enter; he even turned away, but very soon, filled with confusion by his own cowardice, he returned quickly upon his steps, made his way into the banquet-hall, and after confessing his shame, put so much earnestness and fire into his request that everyone desired to cooperate in this pious work.

His bitterest trial however was his father's anger, which remained as violent as ever. Although he had renounced Francis, Bernardone's pride suffered none the less at seeing his mode of life, and whenever he met his son he overwhelmed him with reproaches. The tender heart of Francis was so wrung with sorrow that he resorted to a sort of stratagem for charming away the spell of the paternal imprecations. "Come with me," he said to a beggar, "be to me as a father, and I will give you a part of the alms that I receive. When you see Bernardone curse me, if I say, 'Bless me, my father,' you must sign me with the cross and bless me in his stead."

In the spring of 1208 he finished the restoration of San Damiano. He had been aided by many people of good will, setting the example of work and above all of joy, cheering everybody by his songs and his projects for the future. He spoke with such enthusiasm and contagious warmth of the transformation of his dear chapel, of the grace that God would accord to those who would come there to pray, that later on it was believed that he had spoken of Clare and her holy maidens who were to retire to this place four years later.

This success soon inspired him with the idea of repairing the other sanctuaries in the suburbs of Assisi. Those that had struck him by their state of decay were St. Peter and St. Mary, of the Portiuncula, also called Santa Maria degli Angeli. The former is not otherwise mentioned in his biographies. As to the second, it was to become the true cradle of the Franciscan movement.

This chapel, still standing at the present day after escaping revolutions and earthquakes, is a true Bethel, one of those rare spots in the world on which rests the mystic ladder that joins heaven to earth. There were dreamed some of the noblest dreams that have soothed the pains of humanity. It is not to Assisi in its marvelous basilica that one must go to divine and comprehend St. Francis; one must turn toward Santa Maria degli Angeli at the hours when the stated prayers cease, at the moment when the evening shadows lengthen, when all the fripperies of worship disappear in the obscurity, when all the countryside seems to collect itself to listen to the chime of the distant church bells. Doubtless it was Francis's plan to settle there as a hermit. He dreamed of passing his life there in meditation and silence, keeping up the little church and from time to time inviting a priest there to say mass. Nothing as yet suggested to him that he was in the end to become a religious founder. One of the most interesting aspects of his life is in fact the continual development revealing itself to him. There is hardly anyone, except St. Paul, in whom is found to the same degree the devouring need of being always something more, always something better, and it is so beautiful in both of them only because it is absolutely instinctive.

When he began to restore the Portiuncula his projects hardly went beyond a very narrow horizon. He was preparing himself for a life of penitence rather than a life of activity. But once these works were finished it was impossible that this somewhat selfish and passive manner of achieving his own salvation should satisfy him long. When the repairs were finished meditation occupied the greater part of his days. A Benedictine of the Abbey of Mont Subasio came from time to time to say mass at Santa Maria; these were the bright hours of St. Francis's life. One can imagine with what pious care he prepared himself and with what faith he listened to the divine teachings.

The Portiuncula (lit. "little portion") included the little chapel and land surrounding it—also known as the Church of Our Lady of the Angels (Santa Maria degli Angeli), or simply the church of Saint Mary, located approximately two miles from Assisi, in the plain below the city, near the road that travelers would take to Foligno in one direction, Perugia in the other. In his final days, Francis insisted that his brothers carry his dying body back to his beloved chapel, Portiuncula. (See one early eighteenth-century artist's rendering of Portiuncula below, on p. 153.)

One day—it was probably February 24, 1209—the festival of St. Matthias mass was being celebrated at the Portiuncula. When the priest turned toward him to read the words of Jesus, Francis felt himself overpowered with a profound agitation. He no longer saw the priest; it was Jesus, the Crucified One of San Damiano, who was speaking: "As you go, proclaim the good news, the kingdom of heaven has come near. Cure the sick, raise the dead, cleanse the lepers, cast out demons. You received without payment; give without payment. Take no gold, or silver, or copper in your belts, no bag for your journey, or two tunics, or sandals, or a staff; for laborers deserve their food." These words burst upon him like a revelation, like the answer of Heaven to his sighs and anxieties.

"This is what I want," he cried, "this is what I was seeking. From this day forth I shall set myself with all my strength to put it in practice." Immediately throwing aside his stick, his scrip, his purse, his shoes, he determined immediately to obey, observing to the letter the precepts of the apostolic life.

CHAPTER SIX

First Year of Apostolate
(Spring 1209–Summer 1210)

The very next morning Francis went up to Assisi and began to preach. His words were simple, but they came so straight from the heart that all who heard him were touched. His person, his example, were themselves a sermon, and he spoke only of that which he had himself experienced, proclaiming repentance, the shortness of life, a future retribution, the necessity of arriving at Gospel perfection.

It is not easy to realize how many waiting souls there are in this world. The greater number of people pass through life with souls asleep. Yet the instinct for love and for the divine is only slumbering. The human heart so naturally yearns to offer itself up, that we have only to meet along our pathway someone who, doubting neither himself nor us, demands it without reserve, and we yield it to him at once. The cause of the miserable failure of all the efforts of natural religion is that its founders have not had the courage to lay hold upon the hearts of people. They have not understood the imperious desire for immolation that lies in the depths of every soul, and souls have taken their revenge in not heeding these too lukewarm lovers.

Francis had given himself up too completely not to claim from others an absolute self-renunciation. In the two years and more since he had left the world, the reality and depth of his conversion had shone out in the sight of all; to the scoffings of the early days had gradually succeeded in the minds of many a feeling closely akin to admiration. This feeling inevitably provokes imitation.

"the imperious desire for immolation that lies in the depths of every soul": Chesterton illuminates this brilliantly: "[People] will ask what selfish sort of woman it must have been who ruthlessly exacted tribute in the form of flowers, or what an avaricious creature she can have been to demand solid gold in the form of a ring; just as they ask what cruel kind of God can have demanded sacrifice and self-denial. They will have lost the clue to all that lovers have meant by love; and will not understand that it was because the thing was not demanded that it was done" (CHESTERTON, p. 73).

At Assisi Francis had often enjoyed the hospitality of a rich and prominent man named Bernard of Quintavalle. One day the joy of Francis was very great as he divined Bernard's intentions; he had decided to distribute his goods to the poor and cast in his lot with Francis. The latter desired his friend to pass through a sort of initiation, pointing out to him that what he himself practiced, what he preached, was not his own invention, but that Jesus himself had expressly ordained it in his word.

At early dawn they bent their steps to the St. Nicholas Church, accompanied by another neophyte named Peter, and there, after praying and hearing mass, Francis opened the Gospels that lay on the altar and read to his companions the portion that had decided his own vocation: the words of Jesus sending forth his disciples on their mission.

The early texts actually show Francis less confident and perhaps more spontaneous than is described here by Sabatier. Hearing that Bernard wanted to join him in his life of penitence, Francis told him that it was not easy. His reply then showed a degree of uncertainty as to what should happen next; Francis advised that they go to the bishop's house where there would be a priest, hear mass, and pray until tierce (the third hour after sunrise), at which time they (Francis in his discernment and Bernard after the glow of conversion had naturally dimmed a bit) would open the missal to discover God's will. (See BROWN, *pp. 42–45.)*

"Brothers," he added, "this is our life and our Rule, and that of all who may join us. Go then and do as you have heard."

The persistence with which *The Legend of the Three Companions* relate that Francis consulted the book three times in honor of the Trinity, and that it opened of its own accord at the verses describing the apostolic life, leads to the belief that these passages became the Rule of the new association, if not that very day at least very soon afterward:

If you wish to be perfect, go, sell your possessions, and give the money to the poor, and you will have treasure in heaven; then come, follow me. (Mt. 19:21)

Then Jesus called the twelve together and gave them power and authority over all demons and to cure diseases, and he sent them out to proclaim the kingdom of God and to heal. He said to them, "Take nothing for your journey, no staff, nor bag, nor bread, nor money—not even an extra tunic. Whatever house you enter, stay there, and leave from there. Wherever they do not welcome you, as you are leaving that town shake the dust off your feet as a testimony against them." They departed and went through the villages, bringing the good news and curing diseases everywhere. (Lk. 9:1–6)

Then Jesus told his disciples, "If any want to become my followers, let them deny themselves and take up their cross and follow me. For those who want to save their life will lose it, and those who lose their life for my sake will find it. For what will it profit them if they gain the whole world but forfeit their life? Or what will they give in return for their life?" (Mt. 16:24–26)

At first these verses were hardly more than the official Rule of the Order—(the true Rule was Francis himself)—but they had the great merit of being short and absolute, of promising perfection, and of being taken from the Gospel.

Bernard immediately set to work to distribute his fortune among the poor. Full of joy, his friend was looking on at this act, which had drawn together a crowd, when a priest named Sylvester, who had formerly sold him some stones for the repairs of San Damiano, seeing so much money given away to everyone who applied for it, drew near and said:

Translators of the most authoritative edition of The Legend of the Three Companions *summarize: "Two highly disputed texts,* The Legend of the Three Companions *and* The Assisi Compilation, *reflect the contributions of the three friars who identify themselves in the first text as Brothers Leo, Angelo, and Rufino and in the second text as 'we who were with him.' Both texts provide facts about and insights into Francis not found in the earlier lives and, as such, are indispensable in knowing the details of his life and vision"* (ASSISI, p. 62).

"The missal, which had thus played its part in the creation of the Franciscan order, later came into the possession of Bishop Guido; today it can be seen at the Walters Art Gallery in Baltimore, Maryland" (HOUSE, p. 79).

"Brother, you did not pay me very well for the stones that you bought from me."

Francis had too thoroughly killed every germ of avarice in himself not to be moved to indignation by hearing a priest speak this way. "Here," he said, holding out to him a double handful of coins that he took from Bernard's robe. "Here, are you sufficiently paid now?"

"Quite so," replied Sylvester, somewhat abashed by the murmurs of the bystanders. This picture, in which the characters stand out so strongly, must have taken strong hold upon the memory of those who saw it. It taught them, better than all Francis's preachings, what manner of men these new friars would be.

The distribution finished, they went at once to Portiuncula, where Bernard and Peter built for themselves cabins of boughs, and made themselves tunics like that of Francis. They did not differ much from the garment worn by the peasants, and were of that brown, with its infinite variety of shades, that the Italians call beast color. One finds similar garments today among the shepherds of the most remote parts of the Apennines.

The first brothers lived as did the poor people among whom they so willingly moved. Portiuncula was their favorite church, but it would be a mistake to suppose that they sojourned there for any long periods. It was their place of meeting, nothing more. Their life was that of the Umbrian beggars of the present day, going here and there as fancy dictated, sleeping in haylofts, in leper hospitals, or under the porch of some church.

They went up and down the country, joyfully sowing their seed. It was the beginning of summer, the time when everybody in Umbria is out of doors mowing or turning the grass. The customs of the country have changed little. Walking in the end of May in the fields about Florence, Perugia, or Rieti, one still sees, at nightfall, the bagpipers entering the fields as the mowers seat themselves upon the haycocks for their evening meal. They play a few pieces, and when the train of haymakers returns to the village, followed by the harvest-laden carts, it is they who lead the procession, rending the air with their sharpest strains.

The joyous Penitents who loved to call themselves *Joculatores Domini*, God's *jongleurs*, no doubt often

---

Here is one account of an occasion when Francis ate together with a leper: "A bowl was placed between the two of them. The leper was completely covered with sores and ulcerated, and especially the fingers with which he was eating were deformed and bloody, so that whenever he put them in the bowl, blood dripped into it. Brother Peter and the other brothers saw this, grew very sad, but did not dare say anything out of fear of the holy father. The one who wrote this, saw it and bore witness to it" (ASSISI, p. 167).

---

did the same. They did even better, for not willing to be a charge to anyone, they passed a part of the day in aiding the peasants in their field work. They worked and ate together; field-hands and friars often slept in the same barn; and when at the morrow's dawn the friars went on their way, the hearts of those they left behind had been touched. They were not yet converted, but they knew that not far away, over toward Assisi, were living men who had renounced all worldly goods, and who, consumed with zeal, were going up and down preaching penitence and peace.

We have arrived at the most unique and interesting period in the history of the Franciscans. At the sight of these men—bare-footed, scantily clothed, without money, and yet so happy—people's minds were much divided. Some held them to be mad, others admired them, finding them widely different from the vagrant monks, that plague of Christendom.

When the brothers went up to Assisi to beg from door to door, many refused to give to them, reproaching them with desiring to live on the goods of others after having squandered their own. Many a time they had barely enough not to starve to death. It would even seem that the clergy were not entirely without part in this opposition. The Bishop of Assisi said to Francis one day: "Your way of living without owning anything seems to me very harsh and difficult." "My lord," Francis replied, "if we possessed property we should have need of arms for its defense, for it is the source of quarrels and lawsuits, and the love of God and of one's neighbor usually finds many obstacles in it. This is why we do not desire temporal goods."

The argument was unanswerable, but Guido began to rue the encouragement that he had formerly offered the son of Bernardone. The only counsel that the bishop could give Francis was to come into the ranks of the clergy, or, if asceticism attracted him, to join some already existing monastic order. If the bishop's perplexities were great, those of Francis were hardly less so. He was too acute not to foresee the conflict that threatened to break out between the friars and the clergy. He saw that the enemies of the priests praised him and his companions beyond measure. On the other hand, the families of the Penitents could not forgive them for having distributed their goods among the poor, and attacks came from this direction with all the bitter language and the deep hatred natural to disappointed heirs. From this point of view the brotherhood appeared as a menace to families, and many parents trembled for fear that their sons would join it. As to the clergy, they could not but feel a profound distrust of these lay converters, who, though they aroused the hatred of some interested persons, awakened in more pious souls first astonishment and then admiration. Suddenly to see people without title or diploma succeed brilliantly in the mission that has been officially confided to ourselves, and in which we have made pitiful shipwreck, is cruel torture.

After the death of Francis, some of his followers radicalized his message and actions in their own lives. One of the most colorful of these characters was Angela of Foligno, who cared for lepers with great devotion. Legend has it that she demonstrated her complete trust in God by eating from the sores on the lepers' bodies, saying that she partook of them as if they were the host of the Eucharist itself. Her actions recall the time in Francis's young adult life when he first took to begging alms, forsaking the good food to which he was accustomed in his father's house: "But when he wanted to eat the mixed food offered him, he felt revulsion because he was not accustomed not only to eating such things, but even at looking at them. At last overcoming himself, he began to eat, and it seemed to him that no delicacy had ever tasted so delicious" (THREE, p. 82).

But the more St. Francis was to find himself in contradiction with the clergy of his time, the more he was to believe himself the obedient son of the Church. Confounding the gospel with the teaching of the Church, he was for a good while to border upon heresy, but without ever falling into it. Happy simplicity, thanks to which he had never to take the attitude of revolt!

He resolved, therefore, to undertake a new mission. The *Three Companions* have preserved for us the directions that he gave to his disciples:

"'Let us consider that God in his goodness has not called us merely for our own salvation, but also for that of many people, that we may go through all the world exhorting people, more by our example than by our words, to repent of their sins and bear the commandments in mind. You will find people full of faith, gentleness, and goodness who will receive you and your words with joy, but you will also find others, and in greater numbers—faithless, proud, blasphemers—who will speak evil of you, resisting you and your words. Be resolute to endure everything with patience and humility.'

"Hearing this the brothers began to be agitated. St. Francis said to them: 'Have no fear, for very soon many nobles and learned men will come to you. They will be with you preaching to kings and princes and to a multitude of peoples. Many will be converted to the Lord, all over the world.'"

CHAPTER SEVEN

St. Francis and Innocent III
(Summer 1210)

Seeing the number of his friars increasing daily, Francis decided to write the Rule of the Order and go to Rome to procure its approval by the pope.

This resolution was not lightly taken. It would be a mistake in fact to take Francis for one of those inspired ones who rush into action upon the strength of unexpected revelations, and, thanks to their faith in their own infallibility, overawe the multitude. On the contrary, he was filled with a real humility, and if he believed that God is revealed in prayer he never for that excused himself from the duty of reflection or even from reconsidering his decisions. St. Bonaventure does him great wrong in picturing many of his important resolutions as taken in consequence of dreams; this is to rob his life of its profound originality. Francis was one of those who struggle, and, to use one of the noblest expressions of the Bible, of those who *by their perseverance conquer their souls*. Thus we shall see him continually retouching the Rule of his institute, unceasingly revising it down to the last moment.

The first Rule that he submitted to Rome has not come down to us. We only know that it was extremely simple, and was composed especially of passages from the Gospels. It was doubtless only the repetition of the verses that Francis had read to his first companions, with a few precepts about manual labor and the occupations of the new brothers.

Innocent III had now for twelve years occupied the throne of St. Peter. Still young, energetic, resolute, he enjoyed that superfluity of authority given by success. Coming after the feeble Celestine III, he had been able in a few years to reconquer the temporal domain of the Church, and so to improve the papal influence as almost to realize the theocratic dreams of Gregory VII. He had seen King Pedro of Aragon declaring himself his vassal and laying his crown upon the tomb of the apostles. At the other end of Europe, John Lackland had been obliged to receive his crown from a legate after having sworn homage, fealty, and an annual tribute to the Holy See. Preaching union to the cities and republics of Italy, causing the cry "Italia! Italia!" to resound like the shout of a trumpet, he was the natural representative of the national awakening. Finally, by his efforts to purify the Church, by his indomitable firmness in defending morality and law, he was gaining a moral strength that in times so disquieted was all the more powerful for being so rare.

When Innocent III suppressed ecclesiastical disorders it was less for love of good than for hatred of evil. This priest did not comprehend the great movement of his age—the awakening of love, of poetry, of liberty. He never suspected the unsatisfied longings, the dreams, unreasoning perhaps, but beneficent and divine, that were silently stirring in the depths of people's hearts. He was a believer, but he drew his religion rather from the Old Testament than from the New, and if he often thought of Moses, the leader of his people, nothing reminded him of Jesus, the shepherd of souls.

Celestine III (pope from spring 1191 to January 1198) was already 85 years of age when elected. He is most memorable for his loyalty to Abelard, his former teacher in Paris, when Bernard of Clairvaux led the council of Sens against him (1140). Later, Celestine also petitioned for leniency for Thomas Becket. At the time, "Becket judged him one of the only two incorruptible cardinals" (KELLY, p. 185).

Innocent III's power is perhaps best exemplified in his vow to protect every "citizen" of the Roman Church in the same manner that the ancient emperor Trajan had put fear in the hearts of those who would harm any citizen of Rome. He also excommunicated Emperor Otto IV in 1211.

His reception of Francis furnished to Giotto, the friend of Dante, one of his most striking frescos. The pope, seated on his throne, turns abruptly toward Francis. He frowns, for he does not understand, and yet he makes a real but futile effort to comprehend.

What Francis asked for was simple enough. He claimed no privilege of any sort, but only that the pope would approve of his undertaking to lead a life of absolute conformity to the precepts of the gospel. There is a delicate point here that it is quite worthwhile to see clearly. The pope was not called upon to approve the Rule, since that came from Jesus himself. At the very worst all that he could do would be to lay an ecclesiastical censure upon Francis and his companions for having acted without authority, and to enjoin them to leave

Our image of Francis the saint often obscures Francis the human being. Zofia Kossak's little-known historical novel about the life of Francis and his early followers offers many intriguing hypothetical everyday scenes. Here is a sample glimpse of the debates the brothers might have had while composing the first Rule while traveling to Rome to present it to the pope:

"Elias continued to read:

'And the most important commandment given to the brethren is that they shall love each other. By that sign they will know you for the true disciple of Our Lord, that you shall have love for each other. And every man who shall come to the brethren, be he a thief or a robber, must be welcomed gladly even as he were one of them.'

Brother Elias once more put the parchment down:

'And to this, too, the Holy Father will never agree,' he remarked. 'Why, 'tis pure folly! So if a notorious murderer came to us we should take him in and perhaps even offer him hospitality.'

'Aye,' nodded Francis with conviction. 'Because who knows whether we can't bring him to repent?'

'And he, in the meantime, will rob the brothers and . . .'

'What will he rob them of? What can he do to us? None of us fears death. She is our sister. Only those who possess aught can be robbed. We have naught'" (KOSSAK, pp. 39–40).

to the secular and regular clergy the task of reforming the Church.

Cardinal Giovanni of San Paulo presented Francis and his companions to Innocent III. Naturally, the pope was not sparing of expressions of sympathy, but he also repeated to them the remarks and counsels that they had already heard so often. "My dear children," he said, "your life appears to me too severe. I see indeed that your fervor is too great for any doubt of you to be possible, but I ought to consider those who shall come after you, lest your mode of life should be beyond their strength." Adding a few kind words, he dismissed them without coming to any definite conclusion, promising to consult the cardinals and advising Francis in particular to address himself to God.

Francis's anxiety must have been great. It seemed to him that he had said all that he had to say. For new arguments he had only one resource— prayer. Francis felt his prayer answered when in his conversation with Jesus the parable of poverty came to him. He returned to lay it before the pope:

"There was in the desert a woman who was very poor, but beautiful. A great king, seeing her beauty, desired to take her for his wife, for he thought that by her he should have beautiful children. When the sons were grown, their mother said to them: 'My sons, you have no cause to blush, for you are the sons of the king. Go to his court and he will give you everything you need.'

"When they arrived at the court the king admired their beauty, and finding in them his own likeness he asked: 'Whose sons are you?' And when they replied that they were the sons of a poor woman who lived in the desert the king clasped them to his heart with joy, saying, 'Have no fear, for you are my sons.'"

"Very holy father," added Francis, "I am this poor woman whom God in his love has deigned to make beautiful, and of whom he has been pleased to have lawful sons. The King of Kings has told me that he will provide for all the sons that he may have for me."

So much simplicity, joined with such pious obstinacy, at last conquered Innocent. When Francis heard the words of the supreme pontiff he prostrated himself at his feet, promising the most perfect obedience with all his heart. The pope blessed them, saying: "Go, my brothers, and may God be with you. Preach penitence to everyone according as the Lord may deign to inspire you. Then when the All-Powerful will have made you to multiply and go forward, you will refer again to us. We will concede what you ask, and we may then with greater security accord to you even more than you ask."

Francis and his companions were too little familiar with Roman phraseology to perceive that after all the Holy See had simply consented to suspend judgment in view of the uprightness of their intentions and the purity of their faith. The flowers of clerical rhetoric hid from them the shackles that had been laid upon them. The curia, in fact, was not satisfied with Francis's vow of fidelity; it desired in addition to stamp the Penitents with the seal of the Church. From this time they were all under the spiritual authority of the Roman Church.

The thoroughly lay creation of St. Francis had become in spite of himself an ecclesiastical institution. It would soon degenerate into a clerical institution. All unawares, the Franciscan movement had been unfaithful to its origin. The prophet had abdicated in favor of the priest.

Many scholars argue that Innocent III had two motivations, one noble, the other less so. Innocent had a genuine sympathy with Francis's mind for reform and evangelical poverty. But, he also used Francis and his brothers. By bringing the preaching of the early Franciscans under the shadow and sanction of the Church, Francis helped Innocent defuse the power, and remove the seditiousness, of the Humiliati's and Albigensians' similar ideas.

CHAPTER EIGHT

Rivo-Torto (1210–1211)

Thomas of Celano, very brief as to all that concerns Francis's sojourn in the Eternal City, recounts at full length the lightheartedness of the little band on leaving it. Already it began to be transfigured in their memory—pains, fatigues, fears, disquietude, hesitations were all forgotten. They thought only of the fatherly assurances of the supreme pontiff and promised themselves to make ever new efforts to follow the Rule with fidelity.

Full of these thoughts they set out, without provisions, preaching in such places as they came upon along their route. People hastened from all parts to hear these preachers who were more severe upon themselves than on anyone else. Members of the secular clergy, monks, learned people, rich even, often mingled in the impromptu audiences gathered in the streets and public places. Not all were converted, but it would have been very difficult for any of them to forget this stranger whom they met one day upon their way, and who in a few words had moved them to the very bottom of their hearts with anxiety and fear.

Francis was in truth, as Celano says, the bright morning star. His simple preaching took hold on consciences. "The whole country trembled, the barren land was already covered with a rich harvest, the withered vine began again to blossom."

The greatest crime of our industrial and commercial civilization is that it leaves us a taste only for that which may be bought with money, and makes us overlook the purest and truest joys that are all the time within our reach. "Why," said the God of old Isaiah, "do you spend your money for that which is not bread, and your

"the bright morning star": This phrase originated with Thomas of Celano and became popularly understood in the decades after Francis's death. Dante wrote in his Paradiso that when speaking of Assisi, we might more properly name it "Orient," where the morning star, the Sun, rises. Speaking metaphorically of Francis, Dante wrote: "He was not yet far distant from his rising / Before he had begun to make the earth / Some comfort from his mighty virtue feel" (canto xi).

labor for that which does not satisfy? Listen carefully to me, and eat what is good, and delight yourselves in rich food" (Isa. 55:2). Joys bought with money—noisy, feverish pleasures—are nothing compared with those sweet, quiet, modest but profound, lasting, and peaceful joys, enlarging, not wearying the heart.

In the plain of Assisi, at an hour's walk from the city and near the highway between Perugia and Rome, was a ruinous cottage called Rivo-Torto. A torrent, almost always dry, but capable of becoming terrible in a storm, descends from Mount Subasio and passes beside it. The ruin had no owner; it had served as a leper hospital. Now came Francis and his companions to seek shelter there.

The principal motive for the choice of the place seems to have been the proximity of the Carceri, as the shallow natural grottos are called that are found in the forests, halfway up the side of Mount Subasio. These little hermitages, sufficiently isolated to secure them from disturbance, but near enough to the cities to permit their going there to preach, may be found wherever Francis went. They form, as it were, a series of documents about his life quite as important as the written witnesses. Something of his soul may still be found in these caverns in the Apennine forests. He never separated the contemplative from the active life.

The return of the Brothers to Rivo-Torto was marked by a vast increase in popularity.

Regarding the Carceri, one century-old guide to Assisi writes, "Even to call such shelters huts is giving them too grand a name, for they were but caverns excavated in the rock, scattered here and there in a deep mountain gorge. They can still be seen, unchanged since the days of St. Francis save for the tresses of ivy growing thick, like a curtain, across the entrance, for now there are none to pass in and out to pray there.... [L]ater Franciscan writers...no longer caring to live in caves, only saw Dantesque visions when they thought of these arid, sunburnt rocks, rushing torrents and wild wastes of mountains which even shepherds never reached" (GORDON, p. 84). Visitors to Assisi today may visit Carceri ("the Hermitage"), but it requires a fairly steep hike of about two miles, or a short taxi ride. Francis's own grotto at Carceri is an important place of pilgrimage.

The prejudiced attacks to which they had formerly been subjected were lost in a chorus of praises. But they suffered much; this part of the plain of Assisi is inundated by torrents nearly every autumn, and many times the poor friars, blockaded in the lazaretto, were forced to satisfy their hunger with a few roots from the neighboring fields. The barrack in which they lived was so narrow that, when they were all there at once, they had much difficulty not crowding one another.

When the people of Assisi learned that Francis's Rule had been approved by the pope there was strong excitement. Everyone desired to hear him preach. The clergy were obliged to give way: they offered him the Church of San Giorgio, but this church was manifestly insufficient for the crowds of hearers. It was necessary to open the cathedral to him.

St. Francis rarely said anything especially new. To win hearts he had what is worth more than any arts of oratory—an ardent conviction. He spoke as compelled by the imperious need of kindling others with the flame that burned within himself. When they heard him recall the horrors of war, the crimes of the populace, the laxity of the great, the rapacity that dishonored the Church, the age-long widowhood of Poverty, each person felt taken to task in his or her own conscience.

An attentive or excited crowd is always very impressionable, but this peculiar sensitivity was perhaps stronger in the Middle Ages than at any other time. Nervous disturbances were in the air, and upon people thus prepared the will of the preacher impressed itself in an almost magnetic manner.

To understand what Francis's preaching must have been like we must forget the manners of today and transport ourselves for a moment to the Cathedral of Assisi in the thirteenth century. It is still standing, but the centuries have given to its stones a fine rust of polished bronze that recalls Venice and Titian's tones of ruddy gold. It was new then, and all sparkling with whiteness, with the fine rosy tinge of the stones of Mount Subasio. It had been built by the people of Assisi a few years before; so, when the people thronged into it on their high days, they not only had none of the vague respect for a holy place that, though it has passed into the customs of other countries, still continues to be unknown in Italy, but they felt themselves at home in a palace that they had built for themselves. More than in any other church there they felt themselves at liberty to criticize the preacher, and they had no hesitation in showing him, either by murmurs of dissatisfaction or by applause, just what they thought of his words. These are the conditions under which Francis first entered the pulpit of San Rufino.

His success was startling. The poor felt that they had found a friend, a brother, a champion, almost an avenger. The thoughts that they hardly dared murmur beneath their breath Francis proclaimed at the top of his voice, daring to bid all, without distinction, to repent and love one another. His words were a cry of the heart, an appeal to the consciences of all his fellow citizens, almost recalling

The cathedral of San Rufino dates from around 1000 C.E. It is named for the first bishop of Assisi, who was martyred during one of the Roman persecutions of Christians (238 C.E.). He was drowned in the Chiascio River and his faithful later buried his bones under the high altar. St. Clare was raised in the home directly to the left of the old cathedral, as you stand facing it.

the passionate utterances of the prophets of Israel. Like those witnesses for Yahweh the "little poor man" of Assisi had put on sackcloth and ashes to denounce the iniquities of his people, like theirs was his courage and heroism, like theirs the divine tenderness in his heart.

It was St. Francis who set the example of open-air sermons given in the vernacular, at street corners, in public squares, in the fields. To feel the change that he brought about we must read the sermons of his contemporaries; declamatory, scholastic, subtile, they delighted in the minutiae of exegesis or dogma, serving up refined dissertations on the most obscure texts of the Hebrew Bible, to hearers starving for a simple and wholesome diet.

With Francis, on the contrary, all is incisive, clear, practical. He pays no attention to the precepts of the rhetoricians, he forgets himself completely, thinking only of the end desired, the conversion of souls. And conversion was not in his view something vague and indistinct that must take place only between God and the hearer. No, we will have immediate and practical proofs of conversion. We must give up ill-gotten gains, renounce our enmities, be reconciled with our adversaries.

In Assisi, Francis threw himself into the thick of civil dissension. An agreement in 1202 between the parties who divided the city, following the battles with Perugia, had been wholly ephemeral. The common people were continually demanding new freedoms that

"To understand what Francis's preaching must have been like": Father Cuthbert, in his Life of St. Francis of Assisi, adds: "His language was homely, as it was spoken by the people themselves; he borrowed none of the phrases of the schools: oftentimes the homeliness of the speech was elevated only by the sincerity of the speaker, at other times by the dramatic vividness of the thought or a poetic sensibility to nature" (CUTHBERT, p. 115).

In contrast to the vividness of Francis's preaching, one scholar has summarized that of Pope Innocent III: "These sermons, to the modern reader, are dry...barren.... His preaching shows how scholastic influences had turned the Bible from a book of emotional and ethical truth into a book of scientific truth, and how a vast and minute ecclesiastical polity was hardening and drying the living tissue of the great religious organism" (SEDGWICK, Vol. 1, p. 27).

the nobles and burghers would yield to them only under the pressure of fear. Francis took up the cause of the weak, the *minores*, and succeeded in reconciling them with the rich, the *majores*.

His spiritual family as yet, properly speaking, had no name. Unlike those too hasty spirits that baptize their productions before they have come to light, Francis was waiting for the occasion that would reveal the true name he ought to give it.

One day someone was reading the Rule in his presence. When he came to the passage, "Let the brothers, wherever they may find themselves called to labor or to serve, never take an office that will put them over others, but on the contrary, let them always be under (*sint minores*) all those who may be in the house." These words, *sint minores* of the Rule, after the circumstances then existing in the city, suddenly appeared to him as a providential indication. His institution should be called the Order of the Brothers Minor.

We can imagine the effect of this determination. The saint—for already this magic word had burst forth where he appeared—the saint had spoken. It was he who was about to bring peace to the city, acting as arbiter between the two factions that rent it.

We still possess the document of this *pace civile*, exhumed, so to speak, from the communal archives of Assisi by the learned and pious Antonio Cristofani. The opening lines are as follows:

In the name of God!

May the supreme grace of the Holy Spirit assist us! To the honor of our Lord Jesus Christ, the blessed Virgin Mary, the Emperor Otho, and Duke Leopold.

This is the statute and perpetual agreement between the Majori and Minori of Assisi.

Without common consent there shall never be any sort of alliance either with the pope and his nuncios or legates, or with the emperor, or with the king, or with their nuncios or legates, or with any city or town, or with any important person, except with a common accord they shall do all that there may be to do for the honor, safety, and advantage of the commune of Assisi.

What follows is worthy of the beginning. The lords, in consideration of a small periodical payment, should renounce all feudal rights. The inhabitants of the villages subject to Assisi were put on a par with those of the city, foreigners were protected, and the assessment of taxes was fixed. On Wednesday, November 9, 1210, this agreement was signed and sworn to in the public place of Assisi. It was made in such good faith that exiles were able to return in peace, and from this day we find in the city registers the names of those *émigrés* who, in 1202, had betrayed their city and provoked the disastrous war with Perugia. Francis might well be happy. Love had triumphed, and for several years there were at Assisi neither victors nor vanquished.

CHAPTER NINE

Portiuncula, Early Companions, and Their Work (1211)

Now that they were so numerous the brothers could not continue their wandering life in all respects as in the past. They had need of a permanent shelter and above all of a little chapel. Addressing themselves first in vain to the bishop and then to the canons of San Rufino for the loan of what they needed, they were eventually more fortunate with the abbot of the Benedictines of Mount Subasio. He ceded them in perpetuity the use of a chapel already very dear to their hearts—Santa Maria degli Angeli, or, the Portiuncula.

Francis was enchanted. He saw a mysterious harmony, ordained by God, between the name of the humble sanctuary and that of his Order. The brothers quickly built for themselves a few huts; a quickset hedge served as enclosing wall, and thus in three or four days was organized the first Franciscan convent.

For ten years they were satisfied with this. These ten years are the heroic period of the Order. St. Francis, in full possession of his ideal, sought to inculcate it upon his disciples and succeeded sometimes; but already the too rapid multiplication of the brotherhood provoked some symptoms of relaxation.

The remembrance of the beginning of this period drew from the lips of Thomas of Celano a sort of canticle in honor of the monastic life. It is the burning and untranslatable commentary of the psalmist's cry: "Behold how sweet and pleasant it is to be brothers and to dwell together."

Their cloister was the forest that extended on all sides of Portiuncula, occupying a large part of the plain. There they gathered around their master to receive his spiritual counsels, and there they retired to meditate and pray. It would be a great mistake, however, to suppose that contemplation absorbed them completely during the days that were not consecrated to missionary tours: A part of their time was spent in manual labor.

The intentions of St. Francis have been more misapprehended on this point than on any other. It may be said that nowhere is he more clear than when he ordains that his friars should gain their livelihood by the work of their hands. He never dreamed of creating a mendicant order; he created a laboring order. It is true that we often see him begging and urging his disciples to do the same, but these incidents should not mislead us; they are meant to teach that when a friar arrived in a locale and spent his strength for long days dispensing spiritual bread, he ought not to blush to receive material bread in exchange. To work was the rule, to beg the exception, an exception not at all dishonorable. Did not Jesus and the disciples live on bread given to them? Francis—in his poetic language—gave the name of *mensa Domini*, the table of the Lord, to this table of love around which gathered the little poor ones. The bread of charity is the bread of angels, and it is also that of the birds, which do not reap or gather into barns.

With all his gentleness, Francis knew how to show an inflexible severity toward the idle. He even went so far as to dismiss a friar who refused to work. The Brothers, after entering the Order, were to continue to exercise the calling that they had when in the world, and if they had none they were to learn one. For payment they were to accept only the food that was necessary for them, but in case that was insufficient they might beg. In addition they were naturally permitted to own the instruments of their calling. Brother Ginepro, whose acquaintance we shall make further on, had an awl, and gained his bread wherever he went by mending shoes, and we see St. Clare working even on her deathbed.

This obligation to work with the hands merits all the more to be brought into the light because it was hardly destined to survive St. Francis, and because to it is due in part the original character of the first generation of the Order. Yet this was not the real reason for the existence of the Brothers Minor. Their mission consisted above all in being the spouses of Poverty.

Terrified by the ecclesiastical disorders of the time, haunted by

Chesterton explains Francis's attitude toward asceticism: "It was not self-denial merely in the sense of self-control. It was as positive as a passion; it had all the air of being as positive as a pleasure.... The whole point of him was that the secret of recovering the natural pleasures lay in regarding them in the light of a supernatural pleasure" (CHESTERTON, pp. 73, 64).

painful memories of his past life, Francis saw in money the special instrument of the devil. In moments of excitement he went so far as to execrate it, as if there had been in the metal itself a sort of magical power and secret curse. Money was truly for him the sacrament of evil. He felt that in this respect the Rule could not be too absolute, and that if unfortunately the door was opened to various interpretations of it, there would be no stopping point. The course of events and the periodical convulsions that shook his Order show clearly enough how rightly he judged.

St. Francis renounced everything only that he might better possess everything. The lives of the immense majority of our contemporaries are ruled by the fatal error that the more one possesses the more one enjoys. Our exterior, civil liberties continually increase, but at the same time our inward freedom is taking flight. How many are there among us who are literally possessed by what we possess?

Poverty permitted the brothers to mingle with the poor and speak to them with authority. The ever-thickening barriers that modern life, with its sickly search for useless comfort, has set up between us and nature did not exist for these men, so full of youth and life, eager for wide spaces and the outdoor air. This is what gave Francis and his companions that quick susceptibility to nature that made them thrill in mysterious harmony with her. Their communion with nature was so intimate, so ardent, that Umbria, with the harmonious poetry of its skies, the joyful outburst of its springtime, is still the best document from which to study them.

The originality of St. Francis was brilliant; with him Gospel simplicity reappeared upon the earth. Conversions multiplied with an incredible rapidity. Often, as formerly with Jesus, a look, a word

Sabatier foreshadows the unfortunate interior struggles that ripped apart the Order after Francis's death. The "Spirituals" were pitted against leaders of the Order over the subject of faithfulness to Francis's Rule and ideals regarding living a life of poverty. Raphael Brown summarizes the position of the Spirituals, placing Joachim of Fiore in the equation as he describes "the so-called zelanti, or Spirituals, fanatical Joachimist rigorists and contemplatives who considered the Rule and Testament of St. Francis divinely inspired documents that were equal in rank to the Gospels and were destined to effect in an imminent new age the complete regeneration of the Church and society" (BROWN, pp. 19–20).

sufficed Francis to attach to himself people who would follow him until their death. It is impossible to analyze the best of this eloquence, all made of love, intimate apprehension, and fire. The written word can no more give an idea of it than it can give us an idea of a sonata of Beethoven or a painting by Rembrandt.

The class from which Francis recruited his disciples was still about the same. They were nearly all young men of Assisi and its environs, some the sons of agriculturists, and others nobles; the School and the Church were represented very little among them. Men entered the Order without a novitiate of any sort. It sufficed to say to Francis that they wanted to lead with him a life of evangelical perfection, and to prove it by giving all that they possessed to the poor. The more unpretentious were the neophytes the more tenderness he had for them. Like his Master, he had a partiality for those who were lost, for people whom regular society casts out of its limits, but who with all their crimes and scandals are nearer to sainthood than mediocrities and hypocrites.

Benedict of Nursia's foundational Rule for monks, written about 1,500 years ago, contains similar but softer regulations of poverty, compared to Francis's teachings. Francis's aims were to correct the abuses and laxity that had become commonplace since Benedict, and to follow to the letter the injunctions of Jesus to the first apostles.

In one place, Benedict wrote: "For bedding, a mattress, a blanket, a coverlet and a pillow are enough. The beds should be frequently inspected by the Abbot as a precaution against private possessions. If anyone is found to have anything which was not given him by the Abbot, he is to undergo the severest punishment" (PARRY, p. 87).

The life at Portiuncula must have been very different from that of an ordinary monastery. So much youth, simplicity, and love quickly drew the eyes of people toward it. From all sides they were turned to those thatched huts, where dwelt a spiritual family whose members loved one another more than people love on earth, leading a life of labor, mirth, and devotion. The humble chapel seemed a new Zion destined to enlighten the world, and many in their dreams beheld blind humanity coming to kneel there and recover sight.

Among the first disciples who joined themselves to St. Francis we must mention Brother Sylvester, the first priest who entered the Order, the very same whom we have already seen the day that Bernard of Quintavalle distributed his goods among the poor. Since then he had not had a moment's peace, bitterly reproaching himself for his avarice.

By his age and the nature of the memory he has left behind, Sylvester resembles Brother Bernard. He was what is usually understood by a holy priest, but nothing denotes that he had the truly Franciscan love of great enterprises, distant journeys, perilous missions. Withdrawn into one of the grottos of the Carceri, absorbed in the contemplative life, he gave spiritual counsel to his brothers as occasion served.

The typical Franciscan priest is Brother Leo. The date of his entrance into the Order is not exactly known, but we are probably not far from the truth in placing it about 1214. Of a charming simplicity—tender, affectionate, refined—he was, with Brother Elias, the one who played the noblest part during the obscure years in which the new reform was being elaborated.

We still should say a word concerning two disciples who were always closely united with Brother Leo in the Franciscan memorials—Rufino and Masseo.

Born of a noble family connected with that of St. Clare, Rufino was soon distinguished in the Order for his visions and ecstasies, but his great timidity checked him as soon as he tried to preach. For this reason he is always to be found in the most isolated hermitages—Carceri, Verna, Greccio.

Masseo of Marignano, a small village in the environs of Assisi, was his very opposite. Handsome, well-made, witty, he attracted attention by his fine presence and his great facility of speech. He occupies a special place in popular Franciscan tradition. He deserves it. St. Francis, to test his humility, made Masseo the porter and cook of the hermitage, but in these functions Masseo showed himself to be so perfectly a *Minor* that from that time the master particularly loved to have him for companion in his missionary journeys.

For several years the Brothers Minor traveled from lazaretto to lazaretto, preaching by day in the towns and villages and retiring

---

Rufino, Leo, Angelo (the "three companions" who composed The Legend of the Three Companions)*, and Masseo were four of Francis's closest friends. In both age and spirit, they were like his sons. The four of them were buried near Francis, "at the four corners of his sarcophagus"* (HOUSE, p. 113).

---

at night to these refuges, where they rendered to the lepers, these "patients of God," the most repugnant services. The Crucigeri Order, who took charge of the majority of leper-houses and hospitals, always welcomed these kindly disposed aides, who, far from asking any sort of recompense, were willing to eat whatever the patients might have left. The following narrative shows Francis's love for these unfortunates, and his method with them:

> It happened one time that the Brothers were serving the lepers and the sick in a hospital, near to the place where St. Francis was. Among them was a leper who was so impatient, so unendurable, that everyone believed him to be possessed by the devil, and rightly enough, for he heaped insults and blows upon those who waited upon him. The Brothers would willingly have endured the insults and abuse which he lavished upon them, in order to augment the merit of their patience, but their souls could not consent to hear those which he uttered against Christ and his Mother. They therefore resolved to abandon this leper, but not without having told the whole story exactly to St. Francis, who at that time was dwelling not far away.
>
> When they told him, St. Francis went to the leper, saying, "May God give you peace, my most dear brother."
>
> "And what peace," asked the leper, "can I receive from God, who has taken away my peace and every good thing, and has made my body a mass of stinking and corruption?"
>
> St. Francis said to him: "My brother, be patient, for God gives us diseases in this world for the salvation of our souls, and when we endure them patiently they are a fountain of great merit to us."
>
> "How can I endure patiently pains which torture me day and night? And it is not only my disease that I suffer from, but the friars that you gave me to wait upon me are unendurable, and do not take care of me as they ought."
>
> Then St. Francis took to his knees to pray for the man: "My son, since you are not satisfied with the others, I will wait upon you."
>
> "That is all very well, but what can you do for me more than they?"
>
> "I will do whatever you wish."
>
> "Very well. I wish you to wash me from head to foot, for I smell so badly that I disgust myself."
>
> Then St. Francis made haste to heat some water with many sweet-smelling herbs. He took off the leper's clothes and began to bathe him,

while another brother poured out the water. And behold, wherever St. Francis touched him with his holy hands the leprosy disappeared and the flesh became perfectly sound. And in proportion as the flesh was healed the soul of the wretched man was also healed, and he began to feel a lively sorrow for his sins, and to weep bitterly.

Being completely healed both in body and soul, the man cried with all his might: "I have deserved hell for the abuses and outrages which I have said and done to the brothers, for my impatience and my blasphemies." (See BROWN, no. 25.)

These details show the Umbrian movement, as it appears to me, to be one of the most humble and at the same time the most sincere and practical attempts to realize the kingdom of God on earth. How far removed we are here from the superstitious vulgarity of mechanical devotion, the deceitful miracle-working of certain Catholics; how far also from the commonplace, complacent, quibbling, theorizing Christianity of certain Protestants!

Francis is a mystic for whom no intermediary comes between God and his soul. But his mysticism is that of Jesus leading his disciples to the Tabor of contemplation. When, overflooded with joy, they long to build tabernacles that they may remain on the heights and satiate themselves with the raptures of ecstasy, he says to them, "Fools, you know not what you ask." And directing their gaze to the crowds wandering like sheep having no shepherd, he leads them back to the plain, to the midst of those who moan, who suffer, who blaspheme.

But the higher the moral stature of Francis the more he was exposed to the danger of being understood only by the very few, and disappointed by those

In Palestine, a few miles southeast of Nazareth, Mount Tabor rises nearly 2,000 feet above the Mediterranean Sea. The Hebrew Bible tells how the prophetess Deborah instructed Barak to go up the mountain and wait for Sisera, general of the army of the Canaanites, to approach from below. Sisera, with all of his chariots, fell into the trap as Barak descended Tabor with ten thousand soldiers and slaughtered the armies of Canaan (Judg. 4:1–16). In contrast to this bit of history, Tabor is known for its beauty and is often referred to poetically as a place of contemplation. Tabor is not mentioned by name in the New Testament, but both Cyril of Jerusalem and Jerome, two of the greatest of the early Church fathers, identify it as the place of Christ's Transfiguration.

who were nearest to him. Brother Rufino, for example, the same who was destined to become one of the intimates of Francis's later days, assumed an attitude of revolt shortly after his entrance into the Order. He thought it foolish in Francis when, instead of leaving the friars to give themselves unceasingly to prayer, he sent them out in all directions to wait upon lepers. His own ideal was the life of the hermits of the Thebaide, as it is related in the then popular legends of St. Anthony, St. Paul, St. Pachomius, and others.

Rufino once passed Lent in one of the grottos of the Carceri. Holy Thursday having arrived, Francis, who was also there, summoned all the brothers who were dispersed about the neighborhood, whether in grottos or huts, to observe with him the memories to which this day was consecrated. Rufino refused to come. "For that matter," he added, "I have decided to follow him no longer. I mean to remain here and live solitary, for in this way I shall be more surely saved than by submitting myself to this man and his nonsense."

Young and enthusiastic for the most part, the brothers often found it difficult to keep their work in the background. Agreeing with their master as to fundamentals, they would have liked to make more of a stir, attract public attention by more obvious devotion. There were some among them whom it did not satisfy to be saints, but who also wished to appear such.

Saints Anthony, Paul, and Pachomius were among the first people to become "desert monks" in the third and fourth centuries C.E., leaving cities like Alexandria and Antioch and entering the desert regions of Egypt, Palestine, and Syria to live in caves. The extreme ascetic feats of these people were often compared to those of the athletes of Greece and Rome.

CHAPTER TEN

Brother Francis and Sister Clare

Popular piety in Umbria never separates the memory of St. Francis from that of St. Clare.

Clare was born at Assisi in 1194 and was consequently about twelve years younger than Francis. She belonged to the noble family of the Offreduccio. At the age when a little girl's imagination awakes and stirs, she heard the follies of the son of Bernardone recounted at length. She was sixteen when the saint preached for the first time in the cathedral, suddenly appearing like an angel of peace in a city torn by intense dissentions.

To her his appeals were like a revelation. It seemed as if Francis was speaking for her, that he divined her secret sorrows, her most personal anxieties, and all that was ardent and enthusiastic in the heart of this young girl rushed like a torrent that suddenly finds an outlet into the channel indicated by him. After the sermons of Francis at San Rufino, Clare's decision was speedily taken; she would break away from the trivialities of an idle and luxurious life and make herself the servant of the poor. She sought Francis out and opened her heart to him.

Now, it is one of the privileges of saints to suffer more than other people, for they feel in their more loving hearts the echo of all the sorrows of the world, but they also know joys and delights of which most of us never taste. What an inexpressible song of joy must have burst forth in Francis's heart when he saw Clare on her knees before him, awaiting, with his blessing, the word that would consecrate her life to the gospel ideal.

Francis was too kind to submit Clare to useless tests, too much an idealist to prudently confine himself to custom or arbitrary decorum; as when he founded the Order of Friars, he took counsel only of himself and God. In this was his strength; if he had hesitated, or even if he had simply submitted himself to ecclesiastical rules, he would have been stopped twenty times before he had done anything. Francis, a simple deacon, arrogated to himself the right to receive Clare's vows and admit her to the Order without the briefest novitiate. Such an act ought to have drawn down upon its author all the censures of the Church, but Francis was already one of those powers to whom much is forgiven.

Francis decided that on the night between Palm Sunday and Holy Monday (March 18–19, 1212) Clare should secretly quit the paternal castle and come with two companions to Portiuncula, where he would await her, and would give her the veil. She arrived just as the friars were singing matins. They went out, the story goes, carrying candles in their hands, to meet the bride, while from the woods around Portiuncula resounded songs of joy. Then mass was begun at that same altar where, three years before, Francis had heard the decisive call of Jesus; he was kneeling in the same place, but surrounded now with a whole spiritual family.

Francis's love for Poverty is often characterized in terms of great intimacy. This is especially true in the earliest documents about him. Even Dante writes, in his Paradiso:

*Then day by day more fervently
he loved her.*

*She, reft of her first husband,
scorned, obscure,*

*One thousand and one hundred
years and more,*

*Waited without a suitor till he
came.* (CANTO XI)

It is easy to imagine Clare's emotion. The step that she had just taken was simply heroic, for she knew to what persecutions from her family she was exposing herself, and what she had seen of the life of the Brothers Minor was a sufficient warning of the distresses to which she was exposing herself in espousing poverty. No doubt she interpreted the words of the service in harmony with her own thoughts:

[The Lord] said, "Surely they are my people, children who will not deal falsely"; and he became their savior in all their distress.

It was no messenger or angel but his presence that saved them;

in his love and in his pity he redeemed them." (Isa. 63:8–9a)

Then Francis read again the words of Jesus to his disciples; Clare vowed to conform her life to them; her hair was cut; all was finished. A few moments after, Francis escorted her to a house of Benedictine nuns at an hour's distance where she was to remain provisionally and await the progress of events.

The very next morning Favorino, her father, arrived with a few friends, inveighing, supplicating, abusing everybody. Clare was immovable, showing so much courage that at last they gave up the thought of carrying her off by force.

She was not, however, at the end of her tribulations. A week after Easter, Agnes, her younger sister, joined her, deciding also to serve poverty. Francis received her into the Order. This time the father's fury was horrible. With a band of relatives he invaded the convent, but neither abuse nor blows could subdue this child of fourteen. In spite of Agnes's cries they dragged her away. She fainted, and the little inanimate body suddenly seemed to them so heavy that they abandoned it in the midst of the fields, some laborers looking with pity on the painful scene, until Clare, whose cry God had heard, hastened to succor her sister.

Francis knew that several others were burning to join his two women friends. He set himself to seek out a retreat where they could live under his direction and in all liberty practice the Gospel rule. Francis, who already was their debtor for Portiuncula, once more addressed himself to the Benedictine monks of Mount Subasio. Happy in this new opportunity to render service to one who was the incarnation of popular claims, they gave him the chapel of San Damiano. In this new hermitage, so well adapted for prayer and meditation, Francis installed his spiritual daughters. In this sanctuary, repaired by his own hands, at the feet of the crucifix that had spoken to him, Clare was henceforward to pray. It was the house of God, but it was also in good measure that of Francis.

At this moment Francis no more expected to found a second order than he had desired to found the first one. In installing Clare at San Damiano he was preparing a refuge for those who desired to imitate her and apart from the world practice the gospel rule. But he never thought that the perfection of which he and his disciples were the apostles and missionaries, and which Clare and her companions were to realize in celibacy, was not also practicable in social positions. Whoever was free at heart from all material servitude, whoever decided to live without hoarding, rich people who were willing to labor with their hands and loyally distribute all that they did not consume, poor people who were willing to work and free to resort, in the strict measure of their needs, to the common fund that Francis called "the Lord's table," these were at that time true Franciscans. It was a social revolution.

There was then at that time neither one order nor several. The gospel of the Beatitudes had been found again, and, as twelve centuries before, it could accommodate itself to all situations.

In installing Clare at San Damiano Francis put into her hands the Rule that he had prepared for her, which no doubt resembled that of the brothers save for the precepts with regard to the missionary life. He accompanied it with the plans of himself and his brothers to supply by labor or alms all the needs of Clare and her future companions. In return they also were to work and render to the brothers all the services of which they might be capable. We have seen the zeal that Francis had brought to the task of making the churches worthy of the worship celebrated in them; he could not endure that the linen put to sacred uses should be less than clean. Clare set herself to spinning thread for the altar-cloths and corporals that the brothers undertook to distribute among the poor churches of the district. In addition, during the earlier years, she also nursed the sick whom Francis sent to her, and San Damiano was for some time a sort of hospital.

The Tertiari, or "Third Order," was formally founded by those who came after Francis, although Francis recognized the needs of men and women who, while remaining in the world, nevertheless desired to live in accordance with his strict interpretation of the gospel. The Third Order (still very active today) became the formal organization for Francis's more simple desires that all people—not just those who took solemn vows of celibacy—would follow the true teachings of Jesus. In his simple way, Francis wrote: "Father, all those whom you have given me in the world were yours and you have given them to me. The words that you gave me, I have given to them" (ARMSTRONG, p. 49). Francis "gave" Christ's words to the people most directly through his preaching and, Sabatier argues, did not see it necessary that most people follow him in the sense of joining the Brothers Minor or Sisters of Clare. (See MOORMAN, chap. 5.)

One or two friars, who were called Zealots of the Poor Ladies, were especially charged with the care of the Sisters, making themselves huts beside the chapel, after the model of those of Portiuncula. Francis was also near at hand; a sort of terrace four paces long overlooks the hermitage. Clare made there a tiny garden, and when at twilight she went there to water her flowers she could see Portiuncula standing out against the aureola of the western sky.

But such a situation could not last long. Clare survived Francis nearly twenty-seven years, and thus had time to see the shipwreck of the Franciscan ideal among the brothers, as well as in almost every one of the houses that had at first followed the Rule of San Damiano. Cardinal Ugolini—the future Gregory IX—in particular, took a part in these matters that is very difficult to understand. We see him continually lavishing upon Francis and Clare expressions of affection and admiration that appear to be absolutely sincere. Yet, the Franciscan ideal—regarded as the life of love at which one arrives by freeing him or herself from all servitude to material things—has hardly had a worse adversary.

In the month of May 1228, Gregory IX went to Assisi for the preliminaries of the canonization of St. Francis. Before entering the city he turned out of his way to visit San Damiano and to see Clare, whom he had known for a long time. He represented to her that the state of the times made life impossible to women who possess nothing, and offered her certain properties. As Clare gazed at him in astonishment at this strange proposition, he said, "If it is your vows that prevent you, we will release you from them."

"Holy Father," replied the Franciscan sister, "absolve me of my sins, but I have no desire for a dispensation from following Christ." In these words is mirrored at full length the spiritual daughter of the

The story of Abelard and Heloise was fresh in the minds of late-twelfth-century Europeans. Eighty years before Francis and Clare first met, the scandal of Abelard and Heloise shocked the Western world on many levels: religious, in the academy, and in popular imagination. Their story became the equivalent of today's popular magazine gossip.

Abelard was the most brilliant— and arrogant—philosopher and theologian of the twelfth century. Heloise, his young student, also became his lover, and their amorous encounters even continued after Heloise's admittance to a convent. When word of the relationship reached Heloise's uncle and guardian, he sent thugs to castrate the young scholar. Abelard became a monk himself soon thereafter and was later accused of heresy by the eminent Bernard of Clairvaux.

This story, in all of its tragedy, is similar to that of Francis and Clare only in their affection for each other. But the mutual love between Francis and Clare was entirely filial.

Poverello. She had penetrated to the inmost depths of Francis's heart, and felt herself inflamed with the same passion that burned in him. She remained faithful to him to the end, but we perceive that it was not without difficulty.

San Damiano often echoed with St. Francis's hymns of love and liberty and did not forget him so soon or become an ordinary convent. Clare remained surrounded with the master's early companions: Egidio, Leo, Angelo, and Ginepro never ceased to be assiduous visitors. These true lovers of poverty felt themselves at home there, and took liberties that would elsewhere have given surprise.

One day an English friar, a celebrated theologian, came according to the minister's orders to preach at San Damiano. Suddenly Egidio, though a simple layperson, interrupted him: "Stop, brother, let me speak," he said. And the master of theology, bowing his head, covered himself with his cowl as a sign of obedience, and sat down to listen.

Clare felt great joy in this. It seemed to her that she was once again living in Francis's days. The little coterie was kept up until her death. She expired in the arms of Brothers Leo, Angelo, and Ginepro. In her last sufferings and her dying visions she had the supreme happiness of being surrounded by those who had devoted their lives to the same ideal as she.

After Francis's death, Clare was in some ways a widow. There are hints of loneliness in her few writings, including her Rule for the sisters. She referred to herself as the plantuncula of St. Francis, or "little plant" of his movement, a reference, no doubt intentional in similarity to the Portiuncula, or "little portion," the beloved place where Francis often resided, and where he chose to die.

After Clare died in 1253, the sisters moved from the remote San Damiano to the chapel of San Giorgio, the same place where Francis had been schooled as a boy, and where he first preached in 1209. The Basilica di Santa Clara was built around San Giorgio from 1257 to 1265, and the famous crucifix of San Damiano—the one that had communicated so clearly with Francis—was moved to the chapel of San Giorgio in the new basilica.

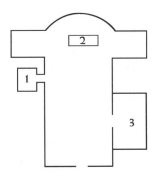

Basic floorplan of Basilica di Santa Clara, as it can be seen today, reproduced after DEAN, p. 9.
1 Chapel of St. Agnes (Clare's younger sister)
2 The high altar
3 Chapel of San Giorgio (also called Chapel of the Crucifix). Clare's tomb is in the crypt below the basilica.

CHAPTER ELEVEN

Francis's Love for All Creatures
(Autumn 1212–Summer 1215)

All eyes were turned toward Syria, where a French knight, Jean of Brienne, had just been declared King of Jerusalem (1210), and toward which were hastening the bands of the Children's Crusade.

The conversion of Francis, radical as it was, giving a new direction to his thoughts and will, had not had power to change the foundation of his character. Francis still remained a knight, and it is perhaps this that won for him in so high a degree the worship of the finest souls of the Middle Ages. There was in him that longing for the unknown, that thirst for adventures and sacrifices, that makes the history of his century so grand and so attractive, in spite of many dark features.

Those who have a genius for religion have generally the privilege of illusion. They never quite see how large the world is. When their faith has moved a mountain they thrill with rapture, like the old Hebrew prophets, and it seems to them that they see the dawning of the day "when the glory of the Lord will appear, when the wolf and the lamb will feed together." We sometimes see that blessed illusion, firing the blood like a generous wine, as these soldiers of righteousness hurl themselves against the most terrific fortresses, believing that these once taken the war will be ended.

*The Children's Crusade was one of the most tragic events of the enormously tragic crusading era of the eleventh to fifteenth centuries. Nineteen years after the death of Saladin, the great Muslim leader, and seven years before Francis's visit to the crusading front, a twelve-year-old shepherd boy named Stephen preached a crusade for children in front of the abbey of Saint-Denis, in France. Philip, the French king, saw the boy but sent him away, failing to anticipate the effect that his young witness would have on the families of France and Germany. While young Stephen told the thousands of young followers who eventually amassed at his side that "The seas would dry up before them, and they would pass, like Moses through the Red Sea, safe to the Holy Land," the reality was that nearly every one of the boys and girls died— several thousand in all—either of hunger and fatigue along the way to the Sea, or aboard ship or in the waters somewhere between Marseilles and Palestine (*RUNCIMAN, pp. 139–43).

Francis had found such joys in his union with poverty that he believed that one needed only to be human to aspire after the same happiness, and that the Saracens would be converted in crowds to the gospel of Jesus, if only it were announced to them in all its simplicity. He therefore left Portiuncula for this new kind of crusade.

It is not known from what port he embarked; it was probably in the autumn of 1212. A tempest having cast the ship upon the coast of Slavonia, he was obliged to resign himself either to remain several months in those parts or to return to Italy. Francis decided to return, but found much difficulty in securing a passage on a ship that was about to sail for Ancona. When the stock of food fell short Francis shared with the sailors the provisions with which his friends had overloaded him.

No sooner had he landed back in Italy than Francis set out on a preaching tour, in which souls responded to his appeals with more eagerness than ever before. One day, Francis and a companion, perhaps Brother Leo, arrived at the chateau of Montefeltro, between Macerata and San Marino. A grand fete was being given for the reception of a new knight and without hesitation they entered the court where all the nobility of the country was assembled. Taking for his text two lines from a popular poem (*Tanto e il bene ch' aspetto* "The happiness that I expect" / *Ch'ogni pena m e diletto* "is so great that all pain is joyful to me"), Francis preached so touching a sermon that several of those present forgot for a moment the party for which they had come.

It was perhaps also during this Lent (spring 1213) that Francis retired to an island in Lake Trasimeno, making a sojourn there that afterward became famous in his legend. But his aim at this time was not to evangelize Italy. His friars were already scattered over it in great numbers. Francis still desired to gain them access to new countries.

Not having been able to reach the infidels in Syria, he resolved to seek them in Morocco. A short time before (July 1212), the troops of the Almohades had met an irreparable defeat in the plains of Tolosa. Beaten by a coalition of the Kings of Aragon, Navarre, and Castile, Mohammed-el-Naser returned to Morocco to die. Francis felt that this victory of arms would be nothing if it were not followed by a peaceful victory of the gospel spirit.

The early biographers are unfortunately most laconic with regard to this expedition. They merely say that on arriving in Spain he was so seriously ill that a return home was imperative. Beyond a few local legends, not very well attested, we possess no other information on the labors of the saint in this country, or upon the route that he followed either in going or returning. But the mission in Spain must have taken place between the Whitsunday of 1214 and that of 1215.

Now we are approaching one of the most obscure periods of his life. Francis seems to have passed through one of those crises of discouragement so frequent with those who long to realize the ideal in this world. Had he seen in the check of his missions to Syria and Morocco a providential indication that he had to change his method? Had he discovered the warning signs of the misfortunes that were to come upon his family? We do not know. But about this time Francis felt the need of turning to St. Clare and Brother Sylvester for counsel on the subject of his doubts and hesitations. Their replies restored to him peace and joy. God, by their mouths, commanded him to continue his apostolate.

Full of joy received through Clare, going on his way southwest from Assisi toward Bevagna, Francis saw some flocks of birds. He turned aside a little from the road to go to them. Far from taking flight, they flocked around him as if to bid him welcome.

"Brother birds," Francis said, "you ought to praise and love your Creator very much. He has given you feathers for clothing, wings for flying, and all that is needful for you. He has made you the noblest of creatures, permits you to live in the pure air, and you neither have to sow or reap; he takes care of you, watches over you, and guides you." Then the birds began to arch their necks, to spread out their wings, to open their beaks, to look at him as if to thank him, while he went up and down in their midst stroking them with the border of his tunic, sending them away at last with his blessing.

On this same tour, passing through Alviano, Francis spoke a few exhortations to the people, but the swallows so filled the air with their chirping that he could not make himself heard. "It is my turn to speak," he said to them. "Little sister swallows, listen to the word of God. Keep silent and be very quiet until I have finished."

We see how Francis's love extended to all creation, how the diffused life shed abroad on all things inspired and moved him. From the sun to the earthworm that we trample under foot, everything breathed in his ear the ineffable sigh of beings that live and suffer and die, and in their life as in their death have a part in the divine work.

"Praised be you, Lord, with all your creatures, especially for my brother Sun that gives us the day and through him you show your light. He is beautiful and radiant with great splendor. Of you, Most High, he is the symbol."

Here again, Francis revives the Hebrew inspiration, the simple and grandiose view of the prophets of Israel. "Praise the Lord!" the royal psalmist sang. "Praise the Lord, fire and frost, snow and mists, stormy winds that do his will, mountains and hills, fruit-trees and cedars, beasts and cattle, creeping things and birds with wings!"

Bonaventure wrote often on the mystical importance of light. All light emanates from a Platonic form of Light, according to Bonaventure. "Light is the substantial form of bodies; by their greater or lesser participation in light, bodies acquire the truth and dignity of their being" (ECO, p. 50).

The day of the birds of Bevagna remained in his memory as one of the most beautiful of his whole life, and though usually so reserved he always loved to tell of it. He felt that he owed to Clare these pure ardors that brought him into a secret and delicious communion with all beings; it was she who had revived him from sadness and hesitation. In his heart he bore an immense gratitude to her who, just when he needed it, had known how to return to him love for love, inspiration for inspiration.

Francis's sympathy for animals, as we see it shining forth here, has none of the sentimentalism that in the poets of the thirteenth century is so often false and affected. In him it was not only true, but had in it something alive, healthy, robust. It is this vein of poetry that awoke Italy to self-consciousness, made her in a few years forget the nightmare of Catharist ideas, and rescued her from pessimism. By it Francis became the forerunner of the artistic movement that preceded the Renaissance, the inspirer of that group of pre-Raphaelites, awkward, grotesque in drawing though at times they were, to whom we turn today with a sort of piety, finding in their ungraceful saints an inner life, a moral feeling that we seek elsewhere in vain.

If the voice of the Poverello of Assisi was so well understood it was because in this matter, as in all others, it was entirely unconventional. How far we are, with him, from the fierce Pharisaic piety of those monks that forbade even the females of animals to enter their monasteries! Francis's notion of chastity in no sense resembles this excessive prudery. One day in Siena he asked for some turtle-doves, and holding them in the skirt of his tunic, he said: "Little sisters, you are simple, innocent, and chaste. Why did you let yourselves be caught? I shall save you from death and have nests made for you so that you may bring forth young and multiply according to the commandment of our Creator." And he went and made nests for them all, and the turtle-doves began to lay eggs and bring up their broods under the eyes of the brothers.

At Rieti a family of red-breasts were the guests of the monastery, and the young birds made marauding expeditions on the very table where the brothers were eating. Not far from there, at Greccio, they brought to Francis a leveret that had been taken alive in a trap. "Come to me, brother leveret," he said to it. And as the poor creature, being set free, ran to him for refuge, he took it up, caressed it, and finally put it on the ground that it might run away. But it returned to him again and again so that Francis was obliged to send it to the neighboring forest before it would consent to return to freedom.

One day Francis was crossing the Lake of Rieti. The man in whose boat he was making the passage offered Francis a fish of uncommon size. Francis accepted it with joy, but to the great amazement of the fisherman put it back in the water, bidding it bless God.

Francis was, like many of us, one who saw the Creator most clearly through the creation. Never a severe ascetic in his theology (he was no John of the Cross), Francis resembled in some ways his later countryman, Dante, who, even on the threshold of the beatific vision in the Paradiso *couldn't for long seem to take his eyes off of Beatrice, his childhood friend and love.*

"Francis was not a lover of nature. He never even uses the word. What Francis loved were birds, flowers, fire, water, animals, and people. He was interested in the concrete: he loved [people], not humanity; wolves, not wildlife; Christ, not Christianity." (CUNNINGHAM 2, p. XII).

We would never be done if we related all the incidents of this kind, for the sentiment of nature was innate with him; it was a perpetual communion that made him love the whole creation. He was ravished with the witchery of great forests; he had the terrors of a child when alone at prayer in a deserted chapel, but he tasted ineffable joy merely in inhaling the perfume of a flower, or gazing into the limpid water of a brook.

The perfect lover of poverty permitted one luxury—he even commanded it at Portiuncula—flowers. The brothers were bidden not to only sow vegetables and useful plants, but to reserve one corner of good ground for our sisters, the flowers of the fields. Francis talked with them also, or rather he replied to them, for their mysterious and gentle language crept into the very depth of his heart.

The thirteenth century was prepared to understand the voice of the Umbrian poet. The sermon to the birds closed the reign of Byzantine art and of the thought of which it was the image. It is the end of dogmatism and authority; very uncertain, no doubt, and to be followed by obstinate reactions, but nonetheless marking a date in the history of the human conscience.

Many among the companions of Francis were too much the children of their century, too thoroughly imbued with its theological and metaphysical methods, to quite understand a sentiment so simple and profound as Francis's love for all creatures. But each in degree felt its charm. Here, Thomas of Celano's language rises to an elevation that we find in no other part of his works, closing with a picture of Francis that makes us think of the Song of Songs:

"Of more than middle height, Francis had a delicate and kindly face, black eyes, a soft and sonorous voice. There was in his whole person a delicacy and grace that made him infinitely lovely. All these characteristics are found in the most ancient portraits."

Fresco painting of Francis from *Sacro Speco* ("holy cave"), the grotto in which St. Benedict lived for a time in the fifth century. A Benedictine abbey still surrounds this place today in Subiaco, Italy. (Art reproduced from SEDGWICK, 1:74.)

CHAPTER TWELVE
His Inner Life and Wonder-Working

The missionary journey, undertaken under the encouragement of St. Clare and so poetically inaugurated by the sermon to the birds of Bevagna, appears to have been a continual triumph for Francis. Legend definitely takes possession of him. Whether he will or not, miracles burst forth under his footsteps. Quite unexpectedly the objects of which he had made use produced marvelous effects; folk came out from the villages in procession to meet him.

One day Brother Masseo desired to put his modesty to the test:

"Everybody follows you, everyone desires to see you, hear you, and obey you, and yet for all that you are neither beautiful, nor learned, nor of noble family. Where does it come from, then, that it should be you whom the world desires to follow?"

On hearing these words the blessed Francis, full of joy, raised his eyes to heaven, and after remaining a long time absorbed in contemplation he knelt, praising and blessing God with great fervor. Then turning toward Masseo, he said, "You wish to know why it is me whom people follow? You wish to know? It is because the eyes of the Most High have willed it. He continually watches the good and the wicked, and as his most holy eyes have not found among sinners any smaller person, not any more insufficient and more sinful, therefore

Masseo was the handsome brother mentioned above (chap. 9, p. 66). Despite his physical beauty and personal grace and charm, Masseo's humility was a delight to Francis. The Little Flowers* tells many stories of Masseo and Francis together. One story depicts the two brothers begging their daily bread while on a journey to France. Masseo went through one street, Francis another. And while Masseo received choice food—fresh bread cut from the loaf—Francis received only meager scraps. The discrepancy only added to Francis's joy, we are told, and the two men blessed the gifts received by Divine Providence.

* The Little Flowers is a collection of short tales from the life and legend of Francis compiled by one Brother Ugolino (not to be confused with Cardinal Ugolino, Francis's contemporary, who became Pope Gregory IX) after the saint's death. First written in Latin, the book was titled Actus Beati Francisci et Sociorum Ejus ("The Deeds of St. Francis and His Companions"), and later abridged and translated into Italian as I Fioretti di San Francesco ("The Little Flowers of St. Francis").

he has chosen me to accomplish the marvelous work that God has undertaken. He chose me because he could find no one more worthless, and he wished here to confound the nobility and grandeur, the strength, beauty, and the learning of this world."

This reply throws a ray of light upon St. Francis's heart. The message that he brought to the world is once again the glad tidings announced to the poor; its purpose is the taking up again of that messianic work that the Virgin of Nazareth caught a glimpse of in her *Magnificat*, that song of love and liberty, the sighs of which breathe the vision of a new social state. He comes to remind the world that the welfare of humanity, the peace of our hearts, the joy of our lives, are neither in money, nor in learning, nor in strength, but in an upright and sincere will.

It was in prayer that Francis found the spiritual strength that he needed; he therefore sought for silence and solitude. If he knew how to do battle in the midst of people in order to win them to the faith, he loved, as Celano says, to fly away like a bird going to make its nest upon a mountain.

With people like Francis, the prayer of the lips, the formulated prayer, is hardly more than an inferior form of true prayer. Even when it is sincere and attentive, and not a mechanical repetition, it is only a

---

The Magnificat, *or "Song of Mary," is one of the loveliest prayers in scripture. It is recorded in Luke's Gospel (1:46–55) and used in public prayer in most Protestant and Catholic liturgical churches:*

> My soul magnifies the Lord,
>
> and my spirit rejoices in God my
>
> Savior,
>
> for he has looked with favor on the
>
> lowliness of his servant.
>
> Surely, from now on all generations
>
> will call me blessed;
>
> for the Mighty One has done great
>
> things for me,
>
> and holy is his name.
>
> His mercy is for those who fear him
>
> from generation to generation.
>
> He has shown strength with his arm;
>
> he has scattered the proud in the
>
> thoughts of their hearts.
>
> He has brought down the powerful
>
> from their thrones,
>
> and lifted up the lowly;
>
> he has filled the hungry with good
>
> things,
>
> and sent the rich away empty.
>
> He has helped his servant Israel,
>
> in remembrance of his mercy,
>
> according to the promise he made to
>
> our ancestors,
>
> to Abraham and to his descendants
>
> forever.

---

prelude for souls not dead of religious materialism. Formulas of prayer are as incapable of speaking the emotions of the soul as model love-letters of speaking the transports of an impassioned heart. To pray is to talk with God, to lift ourselves up to God, to converse with God that God may come down to us. It is an act of meditation, of reflection, that presupposes the effort of all that is most personal in us. Looked at in this sense, prayer is the mother of all freedom. Whether or not it be a soliloquy of the soul with itself, the soliloquy would be none less than the very foundation of a strong individuality.

Now we have come to one of the most delicate features of the life of Francis—his relations with diabolical powers. Customs and ideas have so profoundly changed in all that concerns the existence of the devil and his relations with people, that it is almost impossible to picture to oneself the enormous place that the thought of demons occupied at that time in the minds of people.

The best minds of the Middle Ages believed without a doubt in the existence of the perverse spirit, in his perpetual transformations in an endeavor to tempt people and cause them to fall into his snares. Even in the sixteenth century, Luther, who undermined so many beliefs, had no more doubt of the personal existence of Satan than of sorcery, conjurations, or possessions.

Finding in their souls a wide background of grandeur and wretchedness, from where they sometimes heard a burst of distant harmonies calling them to a higher life, soon to be overpowered by the clamors of the brute, our ancestors could not refrain from seeking the explanation of this duel. They found it in the conflict of the demons with God.

This is how St. Francis, with all people of his time, explained the disquietudes, terrors, and anguish with which his heart was at times assailed, as well as the hopes, consolations, and joys in which his soul was most often bathed. Wherever we follow his steps local tradition has preserved the memory of rude assaults of the tempter that he had to undergo.

Francis believed himself to have many a time fought with the devil, but while for his contemporaries and some of his disciples apparitions, prodigies, and possessions were daily phenomena, for Francis they were exceptional, and remained entirely in the background. In the iconography of St. Benedict, as in that of most of the popular saints, the devil occupies a preponderant place. In that of St. Francis he disappears so completely that in the long series of Giotto's frescos at Assisi the devil is not seen a single time.

In the same way all that is magic and miracle-working occupies in Francis's life an entirely secondary rank. Jesus in the Gospels gave his apostles power to cast out evil spirits, and to heal all sickness and all infirmity. Francis surely took literally these words, which made a part of his Rule. He believed that he could work miracles, and he willed to do so, but his religious thought was too pure to permit him to consider miracles otherwise than as an entirely exceptional means of relieving the sufferings of people. Not once do we see him resorting to miracle to prove his apostolate or to bolster up his ideas. His tact taught him that souls are worthy of being won by better means. This almost complete absence of the marvelous (miracles occupy only ten paragraphs in Celano's first biography of the saint) is all the more remarkable in that it is in absolute contradiction with the tendencies of his time.

Many heretical groups, by contrast, often took advantage of this thirst for the marvelous to dupe the faithful. The Cathars of Moncoul, for example, made a portrait of the Virgin representing her as one-eyed and toothless, saying that in his humility Christ had chosen a very ugly woman for mother. They had no difficulty in healing several cases of disease by its means; the image became famous, was venerated almost everywhere, and

In the early biographies of Francis, we find no mention of some of the popular tales from the Francis legend that are recorded in The Little Flowers, *compiled from oral tradition a century after Francis's death. Modern biographers have debated the accuracy of these stories because many of them go unmentioned in the early lives of Francis. Raphael Brown explains: "How then can we explain the puzzling fact that many of its most interesting stories were not recorded in the first official biographies of the Saint, which were based on the testimony of a number of his companions, including Leo, Angelo, and Rufino? The answer is quite simple. It is really a matter of psychology. The Poverello's best friends would naturally hesitate to mention—and an official biographer would hesitate to describe—a recently canonized Saint of the Church shaking hands with a wolf or eating nothing for forty days or telling his companion to twirl around in a public crossroad or go into a church and preach a sermon while wearing only his breeches"* (BROWN, pp. 27–28).

accomplished many miracles until the day when the heretics divulged the deception to the great scandal of the faithful.

Open the life of Francis's disciple, St. Anthony of Padua (d. 1231) and it is a tiresome catalog of prodigies, healings, resurrections. One would say it was rather the prospectus of some scientist who had invented a new drug than a call to people to conversion and a higher life. It may interest invalids or devotees, but neither the heart nor the conscience is touched by it. It must be said in fairness to Anthony of Padua that his relations with Francis appear to have been very slight.

Among the earliest disciples who had time to fathom their master's thought to the very depths we find traces of this noble disdain of the marvelous. They knew too well that the perfect joy is not to astound the world with miracles, but that it lives in the love that goes even to self-immolation. *Mihi absit gloriari nisi in cruce Domini.* "May I never boast of anything except the cross of our Lord Jesus Christ . . ." (Gal. 6:14). This is, to this day, the motto of the Brothers Minor.

Thus Brother Egidio asked of God the grace not to perform miracles. He saw in them, as in the passion for learning, a snare in which the proud would be taken, and that would distract the Order from its true mission.

St. Francis's miracles are all acts of love. The greater number of them are found in the healing of nervous maladies, those apparently inexplicable disquietudes that are the cruel afflictions of critical times. His gentle glance, at once so compassionate and so strong, that seemed like a messenger from his heart, often sufficed to make those who met it forget their suffering.

Jesus was right in saying that a look sufficed to make one an adulterer. But there is also a look—that of the contemplative Mary, for example—that is worth all sacrifices because it includes them all, because it gives, consecrates, immolates the one who looks. Civilization dulls this power of the glance. A part of the education the world gives us consists in teaching our eyes to deceive, in making them expressionless, in extinguishing their flames.

Thomas of Celano recounts: "A Brother was suffering unspeakable tortures. Sometimes he would roll on the ground, striking against whatever lay in his way, frothing at the mouth, horrible to see. At other times he would become rigid, and again, after remaining stark outstretched for a moment, would roll about in horrible contortions." Francis came to see him and healed him.

But these are exceptions, and the greater part of the time the saint withdrew himself from the entreaties of his companions when they asked miracles at his hands.

"In one of the frescos of the Upper Church of Assisi, Giotto has represented St. Clare and her companions coming out from San Damiano all in tears, to kiss their spiritual father's corpse as it is being carried to its last home. With an artist's liberty he has made the chapel a rich church built of precious marbles.

"Happily the real San Damiano is still there, nestled under some olive-trees like a lark under the heather. It still has its ill-made walls of irregular stones, like those that bound the neighboring fields. Which is the more beautiful, the ideal temple of the artist's fancy, or the poor chapel of reality? No heart will be in doubt.

"Francis's official historians have done for his biography what Giotto did for his little sanctuary. In general, they have done him ill-service. Their embellishments have hidden the real St. Francis, who was, in fact, infinitely nobler than they have made him to be" (SABATIER, p. XXXIII).

CHAPTER THIRTEEN

The Chapter-General of 1217 and the Influence of Ugolino

The four years that followed the Whitsunday of 1216 form a stage in the evolution of the Umbrian movement when Francis was battling for autonomy. We find here rather delicate shades of distinction that have been misunderstood by Church writers as much as by their adversaries. If Francis was sure not to put himself in an attitude of revolt toward the Church hierarchy, he also would not compromise his independence, and he felt that all the privileges that the court of Rome could heap upon him were worth nothing in comparison with freedom.

A great number of legendary anecdotes put Francis's disdain for privileges in the clearest light. Even his dearest friends did not always understand his scruples.

"Do you not see," they said to him one day, "that often the bishops do not permit us to preach, and make us remain several days without doing anything before we are permitted to proclaim the word of God? It would be better to obtain a privilege from the pope, and it would be for the good of souls."

"I would first convert the prelates by humility and respect," he replied quickly. "For when they have seen us humble and respectful toward them, they will beg us to preach and convert the people. As for me, I ask of God no privilege unless it be that I may have none, to be full of respect for all people, and to convert them, as our Rule ordains, more by our example than by our speech."

The question of whether Francis was right or wrong in his antipathy to the privileges of the curia does not come within the domain of history; it is evident that this attitude could not continue long; the Church knows only the faithful and rebels. But the noblest hearts often make a stand at compromises of this kind; they desire that the future should grow out of the past without convulsion and without a crisis.

The chapter of 1217 was notable for the definitive organization of the Franciscan missions. Italy and the other countries were

Sabatier passes over the death of Pope Innocent III in silence. We have the following story, passed down to us through Jacques of Vitry. "On July 11 [1216] the pope had been struck down by an embolism. Because it was very hot, the funeral rites had been rushed; and there was no one to watch over the body in the locked cathedral. The next day, in the early morning, Vitry entered with several members of the Curia and found Innocent III lying naked and stinking on the pavement, all alone in the somber, massive Romanesque church, which still lay shrouded in night. The pope's crosier, tiara, and precious vestments had all been carried off by robbers in the darkness. In a famous letter the French bishop described the horror he witnessed. 'I have seen with my own eyes,' he added, 'how vain, brief, and ephemeral is the glory of this world'" (GREEN, p. 174).

In his novel Saint Francis, *Nikos Kazantzakis tells his story from the perspective of Brother Leo, the book's narrator. Kazantzakis supposes that it was Leo—not Elias, as Sabatier believed—who was Francis's confidant in the early years. In the novel, Leo reminisces to Francis, after the saint's death: "You told me what you told no one else. You took me by the hand, we went into the forests, scrambled up mountains, and you spoke.... I know things about you, therefore, that no other person knows. You committed many more sins than people imagine; you performed many more miracles than people believe"* (KAZANTZAKIS, p. 18).

divided off into a certain number of provinces, each having a provincial minister.

Immediately on his accession, Pope Honorius III had sought to revive the popular zeal for the Crusades. He preached it continuously, appealing to prophecies proclaiming that under his pontificate the Holy Land would be reconquered. The renewal of fervor that ensued, and of which the rebound was felt as far as Germany, had a profound influence on the Brothers Minor. This time Francis, perhaps from humility, did not put himself at the head of the friars charged with a mission to Syria. For a leader he gave them the famous Elias.

This brother, who from this time appears in the foreground of this history, came from the most humble ranks of society. The date and circumstances of his entrance into the Order are unknown, and hence conjecture has come to see in him that friend of the grotto who had been Francis's confidant shortly before his decisive conversion. In his youth he had earned his living in Assisi, making mattresses and teaching a few children to read. Then he spent some time in Bologna, and then suddenly we find him among the Brothers Minor charged with the most difficult missions.

In the inner Franciscan circle, where Leo, Ginepro, Egidio, and many others represent the spirit of freedom, the religion of the humble and the simple, Elias represents the scientific and ecclesiastical spirit, prudence and reason.

He had great success in Syria and received into the Order one of the disciples most dear to Francis, Caesar of Speyer. Later, Caesar was to make the conquest of all southern Germany in less than two years (1221–23), and in the end he sealed with his blood faithfulness to the strict observance of the Rule, which he defended against the attacks of Brother Elias himself.

Caesar of Speyer offers a brilliant example of those suffering souls thirsty for the ideal, so numerous in the thirteenth century, who everywhere went up and down, seeking first in learning, then in the religious life, that which should assuage the mysterious thirst that tortured them.

Brother Elias was deposed in 1239 and soon after excommunicated. He repented on his deathbed, but the century of oral tradition that followed, leading up to Brother Ugolino's compiling of The Little Flowers of St. Francis, *portrayed Elias as not only egomaniacal and despotic, but even demonic.*

Some historians view Brother Elias in a more gentle light. One historian explains: "His successors, Albert of Pisa and Aymon of Faversham, obtained from the Papal Curia seven times as many Bulls, dispensations and privileges as Elias in the whole period of his rule. They decreed that official posts should be reserved for priests, which signified the exclusion of laymen from all government of the Order" (GOAD, pp. 149–50).

Disciple of the scholastic Conrad, he had felt himself overpowered with the desire to reform the Church. While still a layperson he had preached his ideas, not without some success, since a certain number of women of Speyer had begun to lead a new life. However, their husbands disapproving, Caesar was obliged to escape their vengeance by taking refuge in Paris, and then he went to the East where in the preaching of the Brothers Minor he found again his hopes and his dreams. This instance shows how general was the waiting condition of souls when the Franciscan gospel blazed forth, and how its way had been prepared everywhere.

The friars who went to Germany under the leadership of Giovanni of Penna were far from having the success of Elias and his companions. They were completely ignorant of the language of the country that they had undertaken to evangelize. Perhaps Francis had not taken into account the fact that, although Italian might suffice in all the countries bathed by the Mediterranean, this could not be the case in central Europe. The lot of the party going to Hungary was not any better, and for the same reasons. We may thank the Franciscan authors for preserving for us the memory of these setbacks, and not attempting to picture the friars as suddenly knowing all languages by divine inspiration, as was so often done later on.

Francis himself made preparations for going to France. When he arrived at Florence he found Cardinal Ugolino there, sent by the pope as legate to Tuscany to preach the crusade and take all necessary measures for assuring its success. Surely, Francis did not expect the reception that the prelate gave him. Instead of offering encouragement, the cardinal urged him to give up his project:

"I am not willing, my brother, that you should cross the mountains. There are many prelates who ask nothing better than to stir up difficulties for you with the court of Rome. But I and the other cardinals who love your Order desire to protect and aid you, on the condition, however, that you do not leave this province."

"But monsignor," Francis responded, "it would be a great disgrace for me to send my brothers far away while I remain idly here, sharing none of the tribulations that they must undergo."

"Why, then, have you sent your brothers so far away, exposing them to starvation and all sorts of perils?" the cardinal asked.

"Do you think," replied Francis warmly, as if moved by prophetic inspiration, "that God raised up the brothers for the sake of this country alone? God has raised them up for the awakening and the salvation of all people, and they shall win souls not only in the countries of those who believe, but also in the very midst of the infidels."

The surprise and admiration that these words awoke in Ugolino were not enough to make him change his mind. He insisted so strongly that Francis turned back to Portiuncula. Souls thirsty with the longing for sacrifice often have scruples such as these and they refuse the most lawful joys that they may offer them to God. Instead, Brother Pacifico and Brother Agnello of Pisa, later destined to head the first mission to England in 1224, led the missionaries sent into France.

Francis passed the following year (1218) in evangelizing tours in Italy. It is naturally impossible to follow him in these travels,

A fresco painting of Pope Gregory IX (formerly Cardinal Ugolino) in *Sacro Speco* ("holy cave"), the grotto in which St. Benedict lived for a time in the fifth century. A Benedictine abbey still surrounds this place today in Subiaco, Italy. (Art reproduced from SEDGWICK, 1:110.)

the itinerary of which was fixed by his daily inspirations. But it is very possible that he paid a visit to Rome during this time.

Francis's communications with Ugolino were much more frequent than is supposed by the early biographers. We must make a larger place for Ugolino in Francis's story than has been made in the past. At this point in the story, the struggle had definitely opened between the Franciscan ideal—chimerical, perhaps, but sublime—and ecclesiastical policy, to go on until the day when, half in humility, half in discouragement, Francis, heartsick, abdicated the direction of his spiritual family.

Ugolino returned to Rome at the end of 1217. During the following winter he devoted his time to the special study of the question of the new religious orders, and summoned Francis before him. Ugolino, who better than anyone else knew Umbria, Tuscany, Emilia, the March of Ancona, all those regions where the Franciscan preaching had been most successful, was able to judge the power of the new movement and the imperious necessity of directing it. He felt that the best way to allay the prejudices that the pope and the sacred college might have against Francis was to present him before the curia.

At first Francis was much abashed at the thought of preaching before the Vicar of Jesus Christ, but upon the entreaties of his protector he consented, and for greater security he learned by heart what he had to say.

Ugolino himself was not entirely at ease. Thomas of Celano pictures him as devoured with anxiety; he was troubled about Francis, whose artless eloquence ran many a risk in the halls of the Lateran Palace. He was also not without some more personal anxieties, for the failure of his protégé might be most damaging to himself.

Ugolino's anxiety only increased when, on arriving at the feet of the pontiff, Francis forgot all he had intended to say. But Francis frankly admitted it, and seeking a new discourse from the inspiration of the moment, spoke with so much warmth and simplicity that the assembly was won.

The Holy See must have been greatly perplexed by this strange man, whose faith and humility were evident, but whom it was impossible to teach ecclesiastical obedience. St. Dominic happened to be in Rome at the same time and was overwhelmed with favors by the pope. Several years earlier, Innocent III had asked Dominic to choose one of the rules already approved by the Church for his own, and Dominic had adopted that of St. Augustine. Honorius therefore was not sparing of privileges for him. Ugolino surely tried to use the influence of Dominic's example with St. Francis.

The curia saw clearly that Dominic, whose order barely comprised a few dozen members, was not one of the moral powers of the time, but its sentiments toward him were not as mixed as they were with regard to Francis. To unite the two orders would have been singularly pleasing to Ugolino.

An English pilgrim of the late Middle Ages described the relics that he was able to see in the Lateran Basilica in Rome at about this time: "the ark of the covenant, the table of the law, the golden urn of manna ... a tunic made by the Virgin, Christ's purple garment, two bottles of blood and water from His side, the remains of His cradle, the five loaves and two fishes, the Lord's table, and the cloth with which He wiped the feet of the apostles; in addition, the blood of John the Baptist and the ashes from his cremation and his hair-shirt ... and the heads of St. Peter and St. Paul" (PARKS, p. 244).

One day Dominic, by dint of pious insistence, induced Francis to give him his cord, and immediately girded himself with it. "Brother," he said, "I earnestly long that your order and mine might unite to form one sole and same institute in the Church." The Brother Minor wished to remain as he was, and declined the proposition. But so truly was Dominic inspired with the needs of his time and of the Church that less than three years after this, at the chapter held at Bologna in 1220, he was led to transform his Order of Canons of St. Augustine into an order of mendicant monks, whose constitutions were outlined on those of the Franciscans.

A few years later the Dominicans took, so to speak, their revenge, and obliged the Brothers Minor to give learning a large place in their work. Thus, the two religious

"There was a striking contrast between Francis and Dominic, manifest even in their physical appearance. Wearing a garment the color of earth and dust, the Poverello reminded the viewer of a sparrow or, as they were called in France, a moineau—a little monk.... Dominic was altogether different. In his handsome habit of yellow wool so pale it looked white, he had an air of somewhat intimidating nobility" (GREEN, p. 170).

families rivaled each other, impressed and influenced each other, yet never so much as to lose all traces of their origins—summed up for one in poverty and lay preaching, for the other in learning and the preaching of the clergy.

CHAPTER FOURTEEN
St. Dominic and St. Francis

Art and poetry have done well in inseparably associating St. Dominic and St. Francis. The glory of the first is only a reflection of that of the second, and it is in placing them side by side that we succeed best in understanding the genius of the Poverello.

If Francis is the man of inspiration, Dominic is that of obedience—one may say that his life was passed on the road to Rome, where he continually went to ask for instructions. His legend was therefore very slow to be formed; but neither the zeal of Gregory IX for his memory nor the learning of his disciples was able to do for the *Hammer of heretics* what the love of the people did for the *Father of the poor*.

We have already seen the efforts of Cardinal Ugolino to unite the two orders, and the reasons he had for this course. He went to the chapter-general that met at Portiuncula (June 3, 1218), to which also came St. Dominic with several of his disciples. The Brothers Minor went in procession to meet the cardinal, who immediately dismounted from his horse and lavished affection upon them. An altar was set up in the open air, at which he said mass, Francis performing the functions of deacon.

Dominic was amazed at the absence of material cares. Francis had advised his brothers not to trouble themselves in any respect about food and drink; he knew from experience that they might fearlessly trust all that to the love of the neighboring population. The joy of the Franciscans, the sympathy of the people with them, the poverty of the huts of Portiuncula, all this impressed Dominic deeply. So much was he moved by it that in a burst of enthusiasm he announced his resolution to embrace Gospel poverty.

Ugolino, though also moved, did not forget his former anxieties. The Franciscan Order was too large not to include a group of malcontents; a few friars who before their conversions had studied in the universities began to condemn the extreme simplicity laid upon them as a duty. To men no longer sustained by enthusiasm the short precepts of the Rule appeared a charter all too insufficient for a vast association. They turned with envy toward the monumental abbeys of the Benedictines, the regular Canons, the Cistercians, and toward the ancient monastic legislations. They had no difficulty in perceiving in Ugolino a powerful ally, or in confiding their observations to him.

When Ugolino deemed the propitious moment arrived, he made a few suggestions to Francis in a private conversation. Might he give to his disciples, especially to the educated among them, a greater share of the burdens? Might he consult them, gain inspiration from their views? Was there not room to profit from the experience of the older orders? Though all of this was said casually and with the greatest possible tact, Francis felt himself wounded to the quick, and without answering he drew the cardinal into the very midst of the chapter.

"My brothers," he said with fire, "the Lord has called me into the ways of simplicity and humility. In them he has shown me the truth for myself and for those who desire to believe and follow me. Do not, then, come speaking to me of the Rule of St. Benedict, of St. Augustine, of St. Bernard, or of any other, but solely of that which God in his mercy has seen fit to show to me, and of which he has told me that he would, by its means, make a new covenant with the world."

"Francis was of the people and the people recognized themselves in him. He had their poetry and their aspirations. He espoused their claims and the very name of his institute had at first a political signification: in Assisi, as in most other Italian towns, there were majores and minores, the popolo grasso and the popolo minuto. Francis resolutely placed himself among the latter. This political side of his apostolate needs to be clearly apprehended if we would understand its amazing success and the wholly unique character of the Franciscan movement in its beginning" (SABATIER, pp. XVI–XVII).

This warmth in defending and affirming his ideas profoundly astonished Ugolino, who did not add a word. As for Dominic, what he had just seen at Portiuncula was to him a revelation. He felt that his zeal for the Church could not be greater, but he also perceived that he could serve her with more success by certain changes in his weapons.

A few months later, Dominic set out for Spain. The intensity of the crisis through which he passed has not been sufficiently noticed. The religious writers recount at length his sojourn in the grotto of Segovia, but they see only the ascetic practices, the prayers, the genuflections, and do not think of looking for the cause of all this. From this period it might be said that Dominic was unceasingly occupied in copying Francis, if the word did not have such a displeasing sense. When he arrived at Segovia, Dominic followed the example of the Brothers Minor, founding a hermitage in the outskirts of the city, hidden among the rocks that overlook the town, and from there he descended from time to time to preach to the people. The transformation in his mode of life was so evident that several of his companions rebelled and refused to follow him in the new way.

Thus St. Dominic also arrived at the poverty of the gospel. But while Francis had soared to it as on wings, seeing in it the final emancipation from all the anxieties that debase this life, Dominic considered it only as a means; it was for him one more weapon in the arsenal of the host charged with the defense of the Church. But we must not see in this a mere vulgar calculation. Dominic's admiration for him whom he imitated and followed was sincere and profound, but genius is not to be copied. This sacred malady was not his. Dominic has transmitted to his sons a sound and robust blood, thanks to which they have known nothing of those paroxysms of hot fever, those lofty flights, those sudden returns that make the story of the Franciscans the story of the most tempest-tossed society the world has ever known, in which glorious chapters are mingled with pages trivial and grotesque, sometimes even coarse.

Dante's Paradiso *inseparably linked Dominic and Francis. In canto xii, Dante wrote of the changes found in Francis's order after his death:* "His family, that had straight forward moved / With feet upon his footprints, are turned around." *Then, Dante writes, out of the mouth of the spirit of Bonaventure:* "'Twill not be from Casal nor Acquasparta, / From whence come such unto the written word / That one avoids it, and the other narrows'" *(lines 115–16, 124–26).*

As general of the order from 1257 until his death in 1274, Bonaventure sought a "middle way" between the two extremes of the "Spirituals," or strict observers of Francis's original Rule, and those, like Ugolino, who sought to bring the order in line with others, under the Holy See in Rome. When Dante has Bonaventure referring to "Casal nor Acquasparta," he is foretelling the future, referring to Dante's contemporaries, Ubertino of Cassale, a leader of the Spirituals, and Matteo d'Acquasparta, who was general of the order beginning in 1287.

(Ubertino of Cassale is a major character in Umberto Eco's fascinating historical novel The Name of the Rose. *The debates of the Spirituals form much of the intellectual background of the book.)*

CHAPTER FIFTEEN

The Egyptian Mission: Preaching to the Sultan (Summer 1218—Autumn 1220)

At the chapter of 1218, Francis heard the malcontented murmurs of the missionaries that he had sent out the year before to Germany and Hungary. They had returned completely discouraged. The account of the sufferings they had endured produced so great an effect that from that time forward many of the friars added to their prayers this formula: "Lord, preserve us from the heresy of the Lombards and the ferocity of the Germans."

This explains how Ugolino at last succeeded in convincing Francis of his duty to no longer expose his friars to heretics. It was decided that at the end of the next chapter the missionaries should be armed with a papal brief that would serve them as ecclesiastical passport:

> Honorius, bishop, servant of the servants of God, to the archbishops, bishops, abbots, deacons, archdeacons, and other ecclesiastical superiors, salutation and the apostolic blessing.
>
> Our dear son, brother Francis, and his companions of the life and the Order of the Brothers Minor, having renounced the vanities of this world to choose a mode of life that has merited the approval of the Roman Church, and to go out after the example of the Apostles to cast in various regions the seed of the word of God, we pray and exhort you by these apostolic letters to receive as good catholics the friars of the above mentioned society, bearers of these presents, warning you to be favorable to them and treat them with kindness for the honor of God and out of consideration for us.
>
> Given (at Rieti) this third day of the ides of June (June 11, 1219), in the third year of our pontificate.

That summer was the time fixed by Honorius III for making a new effort in the East and directing upon Egypt all the forces of the crusaders. For his part, Francis thought the moment had arrived for realizing the project that he had not been able to execute in 1212.

Strangely enough, Ugolino, who two years before had hindered his going to France, now left him in entire freedom to carry out this new expedition. Francis left Portiuncula in the middle of June and went to Ancona, from where the crusaders were to set sail for Egypt on St. John's Day (June 24).

Many friars joined him—a fact not without its inconveniences for a journey by sea, where they were obliged to depend on the charity of the owners of the boats, or of their fellow travelers. We can understand Francis's embarrassment on arriving at Ancona and finding himself obliged to leave behind a number of those who so earnestly longed to go with him.

We do not know what itinerary they followed. Only a single incident of the journey on the way to the continent has come down to us: the story of the disciplining of Brother Barbaro, guilty of speaking evil against another, on the island of Cyprus. Francis was implacable with regard to loose tongues so customary among pious people, and which often made a hell of religious houses that, on the surface, appeared most peaceful. On this occasion, the offense appeared even more grave because it had been uttered in the presence of a stranger, a knight of that district. The latter was stupefied on hearing Francis command the guilty one to eat a lump of donkey's dung that lay there, adding, "The mouth that has distilled the venom of hatred against my brother must eat this excrement."

The Emperor at this time was, by most accounts, an enemy of the Church and a reluctant crusader. One of the most colorful leaders of the time, Frederick II "was a Norman, raised in Umbria and Sicily as a ward of Pope Innocent III (he was baptized in the same church as St. Francis), intelligent, multilingual, much interested in mathematics and philosophy, acquainted with and respectful of the Muslim religion. Like St. Francis, Frederick was always traveling, but he did not travel lightly. His entourage included a harem, elephants, camels, falcons, a guard of Lucera Saracens, Arab, Greek, and Jewish attendants, doctors and scientists, his crown, his jewels, and a good part of his extensive library" (MARTIN, p. 256).

After years of broken promises to the Holy See, and the public urging of the new pope (Gregory IX, formerly Ugolino, who had such influence over Francis), Frederick II finally left for the Holy Land in 1227, only to disembark fifty miles into his journey. Gregory and Frederick exchanged excommunication and condemnation of each other, and nine months later, Frederick sailed again for Syria. When he arrived, it was not to fight; instead, he negotiated a treaty with the sultan to cede most of Jerusalem, Nazareth, and Bethlehem to the Europeans for ten years, and he hastily returned to Italy.

It is probable that the missionaries debarked at St. Jean d'Acre, arriving there about the middle of July. From the moment that he arrived, Francis was heartbroken with the moral condition of the Christian army. Even with the presence of numerous prelates and the apostolic legate, it was disorganized for want of discipline. He was so affected by this that when there was talk of battle he felt it his duty to advise against it, predicting that the Christians would definitely be beaten. No one heeded him, and on August 29 the crusaders, having attacked the Saracens, were terribly routed.

His predictions won him a marvelous success. In this mass of men from every corner of Europe, the troubled, the seers, the enlightened ones, those who thirsted for righteousness and truth, were elbowed by rascals, adventurers, those who were greedy for gold and plunder, capable of much good or much evil. Loosed from the bonds of family, property, and the habits that usually entwine themselves around a person's will, these men were ready for a complete change in their manner of life. Those among them who were sincere and had come there with generous purposes were, so to speak, predestined to enter the peaceful army of the Brothers Minor. Francis was to win in this mission fellow-laborers who would assure the success of his work in the countries of northern Europe.

In a letter to friends, Jacques of Vitry, the French priest recently appointed bishop of Acre, describes the impression produced on him by Francis:

> I announce to you that Master Reynier, Prior of St. Michael, has entered the Order of the Brothers Minor, an Order that is multiplying rapidly on all sides because it imitates the primitive Church and follows the life of the Apostles in everything. The master of these brothers is named Brother Francis. He is so lovable that he is venerated by everyone. Having come into our army, he has not been afraid, in his zeal for the faith, to go to our enemies. For many days he announced the word of God to the Saracens, but with little success. Then the sultan, King of Egypt, asked him in secret to ask God to reveal to him, by some miracle, which is the best religion.
>
> Colin, the Englishman, our clerk, has entered the same order, as also two more of our companions, Michael and Dom Matthew, to whom I had given the

rectorship of the Sainte Chapelle. Cantor and Henry have done the same, and still others whose names I have forgotten.

For the interviews between Francis and the sultan, it is best to keep to the narratives of Jacques of Vitry and William of Tyre. Although William of Tyre wrote at a comparatively late date (between 1275 and 1295), he wrote as a historian and founded his work on authentic documents. We see that he knows no more than Jacques of Vitry of the proposal said to have been made by Francis to pass through a fire if the priests of Muhammed would do the same, in order to establish the superiority of Christianity.

Sabatier tells us very little of Francis and the sultan. One historian of the Crusades adds: "[Francis] now asked permission of Pelagius [a cardinal of the Church in Spain, sent by Pope Honorius to lead the crusaders] to go to see the Sultan. After some hesitation Pelagius agreed, and sent him under a flag of truce to Fariskur. The Muslim guards were suspicious at first but soon decided that anyone so simple, so gentle and so dirty must be mad, and treated him with the respect due to a man who had been touched by God" (RUNCIMAN, pp. 159–60).

We know how little such an appeal to signs is characteristic of St. Francis. Perhaps the story, which comes from Bonaventure, was born out of a misconception. The sultan, like a new Pharaoh, may have laid it upon the strange preacher to prove his mission by miracles. Either way, Francis and his companions were treated with great consideration, a fact all the more meritorious when you consider that hostilities were then at their height.

Returning to the crusading camp, Francis and his companions remained there until after the taking of Damietta (November 5, 1219). This time the Christians were victorious. Jacques of Vitry relates at length the shocking conditions of the city, where the victors found piled heaps of dead bodies, quarreled over the sharing of booty, and sold the wretched

In Kazantzakis's novel, Brother Leo describes the scene: "Francis ran among the soldiers of Christ and exhorted them with tearful eyes to be merciful, but they drove him away, jeered him, and continued to break down the doors of the houses. How can I ever forget the cries of the women and the groans of the men they slaughtered! The blood ran in rivers; wherever you turned you stumbled over a severed head. The air was thick with moans and wailing" (KAZANTZAKIS, p. 243).

creatures who had not succumbed to pestilence. All these scenes of terror, cruelty, and greed caused Francis profound horror. The human beast was let loose, and the apostle's voice could no more make itself heard in the midst of the savage clamor any more than that of a life-saver over a raging ocean.

Francis set out for Syria and the holy places. We would gladly follow him in this pilgrimage—through Judea and Galilee, to Bethlehem, Nazareth, and Gethsemane—but the documents here suddenly fail us. What was said to him by the stable where the Son of Mary was born, the workshop where he toiled, the olive tree where he accepted the bitter cup? Setting out from Damietta very shortly after the crusader victory at Damietta he may have easily been at Bethlehem by Christmas 1219. But we know nothing, absolutely nothing, except that his sojourn was longer than had been expected.

Angelo Clareno relates that the Sultan of Egypt, touched by Francis's preaching, gave command that he and all his friars should have free access to the Holy Sepulcher without the payment of any tribute.

When Acre (see glossary) fell again into Muslim hands in 1291, the Franciscans fled to Cyprus, where the seat of the province, created in 1217, was located. Officially, Christians were banned from the Holy Land, but the Franciscans remained present, through great persistence, in many ways. In the first half of the fourteenth century, the friars were recognized by the Muslim leaders as "official residents" in the Church of the Holy Sepulcher. At about the same time, Pope Clement VI named the friars as the Church's official custodians of the Holy Land (1342). In 1992, the 650th anniversary of Clement VI's bull, Pope John Paul II reinforced the Franciscans as the Roman Catholic Church's "custodians" of the holy places.

Bartholomew of Pisa, for his part, says that Francis, having gone to preach in Antioch and its environs, caused all of the Benedictines of the Abbey of the Black Mountain, eight miles from Antioch, to give up their property and join the Brothers Minor. These accounts are meager and isolated, to be accepted only with hesitation. On the other hand, we have detailed information of what went on in Italy during Francis's absence.

A plot was laid against Francis by the very people whom he had commissioned to take his place at Portiuncula, if not with the connivance of Rome and the cardinal protector, at least without their opposition. Here are the facts: On July 25, about one month after Francis's departure for Syria, Ugolino, who was at Perugia, laid upon the Sisters of Clare at Florence, Siena, Perugia, and Lucca that which his friend had so obstinately refused for the friars, the Benedictine Rule.

At the same time, St. Dominic, returning from Spain full of new ardor after his retreat in the grotto of Segovia, and fully decided to adopt for his order the rule of poverty, was strongly encouraged in this purpose and overwhelmed with favors. Honorius III saw in him the providential man of the time, the reformer of the monastic orders; he showed him unusual attentions, going so far, for example, as to transfer to him a group of monks belonging to other orders, whom he appointed to act as Dominic's lieutenants on the preaching tours that he believed it to be his duty to undertake, and to serve, under his direction, an apprenticeship in popular preaching.

At the time of his departure for the East, Francis had left two vicars in his place, the Brothers Matthew of Narni and Gregory of Naples. The former was especially charged to remain at Portiuncula to admit postulants, the latter was to pass through Italy to console the brothers.

The two vicars began at once to overturn everything. It is inexplicable how men still under the influence of their first fervor for a Rule that in their freedom they had promised to obey could have dreamed of such innovations if not urged on and upheld by those in high places. Their efforts were bent toward alleviating the vow of poverty and multiplying observances.

It was a trifling matter in appearance, but in reality it was much more, for it was the first movement of the old spirit against the new. It was the effort of people who unconsciously, I am willing to assume, made religion an affair of rite and observance, instead of seeing it, like St. Francis, as the conquest of freedom that makes us free in all things. This is the freedom that leads each soul to obey the divine and mysterious power that the flowers of the fields adore, that the birds of the air bless,

A contemporary biographer of Francis explains: "A rumor had reached the Porziuncula that Francis was dead. As a result many of the newer friars, who didn't know him, had urged his vicars, Matthew and Gregory, to bring the brotherhood more into line with the traditional orders" (HOUSE, p. 218).

that the symphony of the stars praises, and that Jesus of Nazareth called *Abba*, or, Father.

The first Rule was excessively simple on the matter of fasts. The friars were to abstain from meat on Wednesdays and Fridays; they might add Mondays and Saturdays, but only on Francis's special authorization. The two vicars and their followers complicated this rule in a surprising manner. At the chapter-general held in Francis's absence (May 17, 1220), they decided, first, that in times of feasting the friars were not to provide meat, but if it were offered to them spontaneously they were to eat it; second, that all should fast on Mondays as well as Wednesdays and Fridays; third, that on Mondays and Saturdays they should abstain from milk products unless by chance the adherents of the Order brought some to them.

These beginnings bear witness to an effort to imitate the ancient orders, with the vague hope that they would be substituted for them. These modifications of the Rule did not pass, however, without arousing the indignation of a part of the chapter. A lay brother made himself their eager messenger and set out for the East to entreat Francis to return without delay.

There were also other causes of disquiet. A certain Brother Giovanni of Conpello had gathered together a great number of lepers of both sexes and written a rule, intending to form with them a new order. He had afterward presented himself before the supreme pontiff with a train of these unfortunates to obtain his approbation. The report of Francis's death had even been spread abroad, so that the whole Order was disturbed, divided, and in the greatest peril. The dark presentiments that Francis seems to have had were exceeded by the reality. The messenger who brought him the sad news found him in Syria, probably at St. Jean d'Acre. Francis embarked at once with Elias, Peter of Catana, Caesar of Speyer, and a few others, and returned to Italy in a vessel bound for Venice.

CHAPTER SIXTEEN
Crisis in the Order (Autumn 1220)

On his arrival in Venice, Francis informed himself more exactly concerning all that had happened, and convoked the chapter-general at Portiuncula for Michaelmas (September 29, 1220). His first care was doubtless to reassure his sister-friend at San Damiano. A short fragment of a letter that has been preserved to us gives indication of the sad anxieties that filled his mind:

> I, little Brother Francis, desire to follow the life and the poverty of Jesus Christ, our most high Lord, and of his most holy Mother, persevering in it until the end. And I beg you all and exhort you to persevere always in this most holy life and poverty, and take good care never to depart from it upon the advice or teachings of any one at all.

A long shout of joy sounded up and down all Italy when the news of his return was heard. Many zealous brothers were already despairing, for persecutions had begun in many provinces. So, when they learned that their spiritual father was alive and coming again to visit them their joy was unbounded.

From Venice, Francis went to Bologna. The journey was marked by an incident that once more shows his acute and wise goodness. Worn out as much by emotion as by fatigue, one day he found himself obliged to give up finishing the journey on foot. Mounted on a donkey, he was going on his way followed by Brother Leonard of Assisi, when a passing glance showed him what was passing in his companion's mind. "My relatives," the friar was thinking, "would have been far from associating with Bernardone, and yet here I am, obliged to follow his son on foot."

Imagine Brother Leonard's astonishment when he heard Francis saying, as he hastily dismounted from his beast: "Here, take my place. You shouldn't follow me on foot, as you are of a noble and powerful lineage." The unhappy Leonard, much confused, threw himself at Francis's feet, begging for pardon.

The Bolognese prepared an enthusiastic reception for Francis, an account of which has come down even to our times:

I was studying at Bologna, I, Thomas of Spalato, archdeacon in the cathedral church of that city, when in the year 1220, the day of the Assumption, I saw St. Francis preaching on the piazza of the Lesser Palace, before almost every person in the city. The theme of the discourse was the following: Angels, people, the demons. He spoke on all these subjects with so much wisdom and eloquence that many learned people who were there were filled with admiration at the words of so plain a man. His ways were those of conversation; the substance of his discourse rested mainly upon the abolition of enmities and the necessity of making peaceful alliances. His apparel was poor, his person in no respect imposing, his face not at all handsome, but God gave such great efficacy to his words that he brought back to peace and harmony many nobles whose savage fury had even led to the shedding of blood. So great a devotion was felt for him that men and women flocked after him, and they esteemed themselves happy who succeeded in touching the hem of his garment.

Francis remained in Bologna only a very short time. An ancient tradition, of which his biographers have not preserved a trace but nevertheless appears to be entirely probable, says that Ugolino took him to pass a month in the Camaldoli. This retreat was formerly inhabited by St. Romuald, in the midst of the Casentino forest, one of the noblest in Europe, and within a few hours walk of the Verna, whose summit rises up gigantic, overlooking the whole country.

St. Dominic's tomb is housed in Bologna in a basilica named for him. On the cornice of the tomb are statues of the eight patron saints of Bologna, among them, St. Francis and St. Dominic, as well as St. Petronius (early fifth-century bishop of Bologna) and St. Procolus (early Christian martyr, martyred in Bologna), the latter two carved by Michelangelo in 1494. The Basilica also contains the beautiful fresco, Apotheosis of St. Dominic, by Guido Reni.

We know how much Francis needed repose. There is no doubt that he also longed for a period of meditation in order to decide carefully in advance on his line of conduct, in the midst of the dark conjectures that had called him home.

The desire to give him a much-needed rest was only a subordinate purpose with Ugolino. We can easily picture his responses to Francis's complaints. The Brothers

Minor were not heretics, but they disturbed the Church as much as the heretics did. How many times had Francis been reminded that a great association, in order to exist, must have precise and detailed regulations? Of course Francis's humility was doubted by no one, but why not manifest it, not only in costume and manner of living, but in all his acts? He thought himself obeying God in defending his own inspiration, but does not the Church speak in the name of God? He desired to be a man of the gospel, but was not the best way of becoming an apostolic man to obey the Roman pontiff, the successor of Peter? Reproaches such as these, mingled with professions of love and admiration on the part of the prelate, must have profoundly disturbed a sensitive heart like that of Francis. His conscience bore him good witness, but with the modesty of a noble mind he was ready enough to think that he might have made many mistakes.

The sojourn at Camaldoli was prolonged until the middle of September and it ended to the cardinal's satisfaction. Francis decided to go directly to the pope, then at Orvieto, with the request that Ugolino should be given him as official protector entrusted with the direction of the Order.

A dream that Francis had once had recurred to his memory: He had seen a little black hen that, in spite of her efforts, was not able to spread her wings over her whole brood. The poor hen was himself, the chickens were the friars. This dream was a providential indication commanding him to seek for them a mother under whose wings they could all find a place, and who could defend them against the birds of prey. At least so he thought.

Does his profound humility, with the feeling of culpability that Ugolino had awakened in him, suffice to explain his attitude with regard to the pope, or might we suppose that he had a vague thought of abdicating? The scene has been preserved for us:

> Not daring to present himself in the apartments of so great a prince, he remained outside before the door, patiently waiting until the pope should come out. When he appeared, St. Francis made a reverence and said: "Father Pope, may God give you peace." "May God bless you, my son," he replied. "My lord," Francis said, "you are great and often absorbed by great affairs. Poor friars cannot come and talk with you as often as they need to

do. You have given me many popes, but give me a single one to whom I may address myself when need arises, and who will listen in your stead, discussing my affairs and those of the Order." "Whom do you wish I should give you, my son?" "The Bishop of Ostia." And he gave him to him.

Conferences with Ugolino began. He immediately accorded Francis some amends: The privilege granted the Sisters of Clare was revoked; Giovanni of Conpello was informed that he had nothing to hope for from the curia; and leave was given to Francis himself to compose the Rule of the Order. At the same time, a bull was issued—not merely for the sake of publishing this ordinance but especially to mark in a solemn manner the commencement of a new era in the relations between the Church and the Franciscans—the fraternity of the Umbrian Penitents became an Order in the strictest sense of the word.

From this time it became impossible for Francis to remain minister general. He felt it himself. Heartbroken, soul-sick, he would have found in the energy of his love those words, those glances that up to this time had taken the place of rule or constitution, giving to his earliest companions the intuition of what they ought to do and the strength to accomplish it. But an administrator was now needed at the head of this family that he suddenly found to be so different from what it had been a few years before.

The recent events had not taken place without in some degree weakening his moral personality;

One of the few writings of Francis to exist in the original is a letter to his dear friend, Brother Leo, with whom he so often traveled the countryside of Umbria, as told in the beautiful stories of The Little Flowers. *It was probably written at about this time, in response to a query from Leo asking whom he should follow, Francis, or the new leaders of the Order. "Brother Leo, brother Francis sends you health and peace. My son, I speak to you now just as a mother would. All the words which we have exchanged in our travels I can sum up in a single word of advice; in this way it will not be necessary for you to search me out for further advice. Here is my advice: Whatever seems right for you to do to better serve the Lord and to follow in his footsteps and in his poverty, do it with God's blessing and my approval. But if it seems necessary for your soul or your consolation to come and see me, and you want to come, then come. Do, I beg you, come"* (CUNNINGHAM 2, p. 162; see also SABATIER, pp. 261–62).

---

from being continually talked to about obedience, submission, humility, a certain obscurity had come over this luminous soul. Inspiration no longer came to it with the certainty of other days. The prophet had begun to waver, almost to doubt himself and his mission. He pictured to himself the chapter that he was about to open—the attack, the criticisms that would be its object—and labored to convince himself that if he did not endure them with joy he was not a true Brother Minor. He resolved then to put the direction of the Order into the hands of Peter of Catana. It is evident that there was nothing spontaneous in this decision, and the fact that this brother was a doctor of laws and belonged to the nobility squarely argues the transformation of the Franciscan institute.

At the chapter-general that followed, nothing reveals the demoralized state of Francis better than the decision taken to drop out one of the essential passages of the old Rule, one of his three fundamental precepts, beginning with these words: "Carry nothing with you." How did they go to work to obtain from Francis this concession which a little while before he would have looked on as a denial of his call, a refusal to accept in its integrity the message that Jesus had addressed to him?

Something of Francis's pain has passed into the touching narrative of his abdication that the early biographers have given us:

> "From here forward," he said to the friars, "I am dead for you, but here is Brother Peter of Catana, whom you and I will all obey." And prostrating himself before him he promised him obedience and submission. The friars could not restrain their tears when they saw themselves becoming in some sort orphans, but Francis arose, and, clasping his hands, with eyes upraised to heaven, said: "Lord, I return to you this family that you have confided to me. Now, as you know, most sweet Jesus, I have no longer strength or ability to keep on caring for them. I confide them therefore, to the ministers. May they be responsible before you at the day of judgment if any brother, by their negligence or bad example, or by a too severe discipline, should ever wander away."

The functions of Peter of Catana were destined to continue only a very short time. He died on March 10, 1221. During this period of a few months, Francis remained at Portiuncula, and desirous of showing himself submissive, he nevertheless found himself tormented by the desire to shake off his chains and fly away as in former days, to live and breathe in God alone. The following, somewhat lengthy, incident says plenty about Francis and the brothers at this time:

One day a novice who could read the psalter, though not without difficulty, obtained from the minister general—that is to say, from the vicar of St. Francis—permission to have one. But as he had learned that Francis desired the brothers to be covetous neither of learning or for books, he would not take his psalter without his consent.

"Father," the novice said to St. Francis, "it would be a great consolation to have a psalter. Though the minister general has authorized me to get it, I would not have it unknown to you."

"Look at the Emperor Charles," Francis replied with fire. "Roland and Oliver and all the paladins, valorous heroes and gallant knights who gained their famous victories in fighting infidels, in toiling and laboring even unto death! The holy martyrs also have chosen to die in the midst of battle for the faith of Christ! But now there are many of those who aspire to merit honor and glory simply by relating their feats. Yes, among us also there are many who expect to receive glory and honor by reciting and preaching the works of the saints, as if they had done them themselves!"

A few days later, St. Francis was sitting before the fire when the novice drew near to speak with him again about his psalter. "When you have your psalter," Francis said to him, "you will want a breviary, and when you have a breviary you will seat yourself in a pulpit like a great prelate and will beckon to your companion, 'Bring me my breviary!'"

Francis's love for poverty, and hate of pride, were two reasons for his strong opinion about the brothers not possessing books. But it is also worth noting that books, before paper, were extravagantly expensive. For example, more than two hundred years after the time of Francis, "It had been calculated that each copy of the Gutenberg Bible (641 leaves) printed on parchment required the skins of 300 sheep" (Hugh Kennedy, in Times Literary Supplement, *August 16, 2002).*

In Francis's Rule of 1221, composed soon after the time of his exchange with the young friar over the psalter, after he had relinquished control of his Order, Francis acquiesced: "The clergy may have only such books as are necessary for their office, and the laymen who can read may be allowed to possess a psalter."

St. Francis said this with great vivacity. Then, taking up some ashes he scattered them over the head of the novice, repeating: "There is the breviary! There is the breviary!"

Several days later, Francis was walking up and down along the road-side not far from his cell when the same Brother came again to speak to him about his psalter. "Very well, go on," Francis said, "you have only to do what your minister tells you." At these words, the novice went away, but Francis, reflecting on what he had said, called to the friar, crying, "Wait for me!" When Francis had caught up with him, he said, "Retrace your steps a little way, I beg you. Where was I when I told you to do whatever your minister told you as to the psalter?" Then, falling on his knees on the spot pointed out by the friar, Francis prostrated himself at his feet, crying, "Pardon, my brother, pardon, for he who would be Brother Minor ought to have nothing but his clothing!"

CHAPTER SEVENTEEN
Francis's Doubts and Weaknesses

The evolution of the Order hurried on with a rapidity that nothing was strong enough to check. The creation of ministers among the Brothers Minor, done in the chapter of 1221, was an enormous step.

Ministers need residences; those who command must have subordinates within reach; and the Brothers, therefore, could no longer do without friaries. This change naturally brought about many others.

Up to this time they were only itinerant preachers, having no need for churches. They were, as Francis had wished, the friendly auxiliaries of the clergy. With churches it was inevitable that they would first fatally aspire to preach in them and attract a crowd to them, and then in some way erect them into counter parishes (counter to the secular churches, or, those not run by members of monastic orders).

The bull of March 22, 1222, shows us the papacy hastening these transformations with all of its power. The pontiff accords to Brother Francis and the other friars the privilege of celebrating the sacred mysteries in their churches in times of interdict, on the natural condition of not ringing the bells, or closing the door, and previously expelling those who were excommunicated. In 1222, it appears that the Order as yet had no "times of interdict," but it is not difficult to see in the pontiff's actions a pressing invitation to change their way of working, leaving this privilege to be availed later.

Another document of the same time shows a like purpose, though manifested in another direction. By the bull *Ex parte* of March 29, 1222, Honorius III laid upon the Preachers and Minors of Lisbon conjointly a singularly delicate mission. He gave them full powers to proceed against the bishop and clergy of that city, who were exacting from the faithful one-third of their property, to be left to them by will, refusing the Church's burial service to those who disobeyed. The fact that the pope committed to the brothers the care of choosing what measures they should take proves how anxious they were in Rome to forget the object for which the brothers had been created, and to transform them into deputies of the Holy See. We perceive here the influence of Ugolino, who refounded the Brothers Minor after his own heart in the person of Elias.

What was Francis doing all this time? We have no clear evidence, but he had probably left Portiuncula and gone to live in one of those Umbrian hermitages that always had such a strong attachment for him. There is hardly a hill in central Italy that has not preserved some memento of him. It would be hard to walk half a day between Florence and Rome without coming upon some hut on a hillside bearing his name or that of one of his disciples.

There was a time when these huts were inhabited, when in these leafy booths Egidio, Masseo, Bernard, Sylvester, Ginepro, and many others whose names history has forgotten, received visits from their spiritual father. They gave Francis love for love and consolation for consolation. His poor heart had great need of both, for in his long, sleepless nights it had come to him at times to hear strange voices. Weariness and regret were laying hold of him, and looking over the past Francis was almost driven to doubt himself, his Lady Poverty, and everything.

Two and a half months after the untimely death of Peter of Catana, Brother Elias, the new vicar of the Order, presided over the Whitsunday chapter of May 30, 1221. "About three thousand friars were there assembled, but so great was the eagerness of the people of the neighborhood to bring provisions, that after a session of seven days they were obliged to remain two days longer to eat up all that had been brought. The sessions were presided over by Brother Elias, Francis sitting at his feet and pulling at his robe when there was anything that he wished to have put before the brothers" (SABATIER, p. 265).

Between Chiusi and Radicofani—an hour's walk from the village of Sartiano—a few brothers made a shelter that served them as a hermitage, with a little cabin for Francis in a retired spot. There he passed one of the most agonizing nights of his life. The thought that he had exaggerated the virtue of asceticism and not counted enough upon the mercy of God assailed him, and suddenly he came to regret what he had done with his life. A picture of what he might have been, of the tranquil and happy home that might have been his, rose up before him in such living colors that he felt himself giving way. In vain he disciplined himself with his hempen girdle until the blood came, but the vision would not leave.

It was midwinter and a heavy fall of snow covered the ground. He rushed out without his garment and, gathering up great heaps of snow, began to make a row of images. "See," he said, "here is your wife, and behind her are two sons and two daughters, with the servant and the maid carrying all the baggage." With this child-like representation of the tyranny of material cares that he had escaped, Francis finally put away the temptation.

There is nothing to show whether or not we should fix at the same time another incident that legend gives us taking place at Sartiano. One day, a brother whom Francis asked, "From where did you come?" replied, "From your cell." This simple answer was enough to make the vehement lover of Poverty refuse to occupy it again. "Foxes have holes," he loved to repeat, "and the birds of the air have nests, but the Son of Man had nowhere to lay his head. When the Lord spent forty days and forty nights praying and fast-ing in the desert, he built himself neither cell or house, but made the side of a rock his shelter."

It would be a mistake to think, as some have done, that as time went on Francis changed his point of view. Certain ecclesiastical writers have assumed that since he desired the multiplication of his Order, he for that very reason consented to its transformation. The suggestion is specious, but in this matter we are not left to conjec-ture; almost everything that was done in the Order after 1221 was done either without Francis's knowledge or against his will. If one were inclined to doubt this, it would only be necessary to read that most solemn and most adequate manifesto of Francis's thought—his will. In it, he is shown freed from all the temptations that had at times made him hesitate in the expression of his primitive ideal, and set it up in opposition to all the concessions that had been wrung from his weakness.

Francis's will may be seen almost as a revocation of the Rule written in 1223. But, it would be a mistake to see in it the first attempt made to return to the early ideal. The last five years of his life were one incessant effort at protest, both by his example and his words.

CHAPTER EIGHTEEN
The Brothers Minor and Learning
(1222–1223)

In 1222, Francis addressed a letter filled with sad forebodings to his brothers in Bologna. In that city, where the Dominicans were occupied with making a stronghold for themselves, the Brothers Minor were more than anywhere else tempted to forsake the way of simplicity and poverty. Francis's warnings put on such dark and threatening colors that, after the famous earthquake of December 23, 1222, which spread terror over all of northern Italy, there was no hesitation in believing that he had predicted the catastrophe.

He had indeed predicted a catastrophe that was nonetheless horrible for being entirely moral, and the vision of which forced from him the most bitter imprecations:

> Lord Jesus, you chose your apostles to the number of twelve, and if one of them did betray you, the others, remaining united to you, preached your holy gospel, filled with one and the same inspiration. Behold now, remembering those former days, you have raised up the religion of the brothers in order to uphold faith, and by them the mystery of your gospel may be accomplished. Who will take their place if, instead of fulfilling their mission and being shining examples for all, they are seen to give themselves up

Seismic activity has always been common throughout Italy. Most recently, on September 26, 1997, two friars and two art experts were killed in Assisi when portions of the ceiling of the basilica, including famous frescos by Giotto, Cimabue, and others, crashed to the floor. Scenes of this were seen on television around the world. Tremors continued throughout October of that year, injuring others and leaving thousands homeless. An October 31 letter that year from a Franciscan pilgrimage program leader in Milwaukee, and a visit to Assisi by Pope John Paul II on January 3, 1998, helped to draw thousands of pilgrims to Assisi, many of whom helped in rebuilding efforts throughout the city, most of which was completed by early 2001.

Art historians have warned that the severity of the earthquake damage to the Assisi frescos could have been lessened if it were not for structural changes made to the building a few decades before, when concrete beams were added to the roof in place of ancient wooden ones. This practice has been fairly common in recent years, including in Padua, where the Scrovegni Chapel contains some of Giotto's most beautiful frescos.

to works of darkness? Oh, may they be accursed by you, Lord, and by all the court of heaven, and by me, your unworthy servant, they who by their bad example overturn and destroy all that you did in the beginning and cease not to do by the holy brothers of this order.

This passage from Thomas of Celano, the most moderate of the early biographers, shows to what a pitch of vehemence and indignation the gentle Francis could be worked up. In spite of natural efforts to throw a veil of reserve over the anguish of the founder, we find traces of it at every step. "The time will come," he said one day, "when our order will so have lost all good renown that its members will be ashamed to show themselves by daylight."

Francis believed his sons to be attacked with two maladies: unfaithful at once to poverty and humility. But perhaps he dreaded for them the demon of learning more than the temptation of riches. He had no difficulty in seeing that there will always be enough students for the universities, and that if scientific effort is a homage to God, there is no risk of a lack of this sort of worshiper. But Francis looked in vain about him for those who would fulfill the mission of love and humility reserved for his order, if the friars were to be unfaithful to it.

So there was more in his anguish than the grief of seeing his hopes confounded. The defeat of an army is nothing compared with the overthrow of an idea, and in him an idea had been incarnated—the idea of peace and happiness restored to humankind by the victory of love over the trammels of material things.

By an ineffable mystery he felt himself to be one by whom humanity yearns to be renewed—to use the language of the Gospel, born again. In this lies his true beauty.

A generation after Francis's death, under Bonaventure's leadership of the Brothers Minor, "The typical friar was to be no longer the wandering evangelist who worked in the fields, tended the sick, slept in barns and churches, a simple, devout, homely soul content to take the lowest place and be idiota et subditus omnibus, but a member of a religious house, well educated and well trained, a preacher and director of souls, a man whom the community could respect and whose services would be valued. In bringing about this change S. Bonaventura set the friars on the road which they were henceforth to travel. It is, therefore, not without reason that he has been called 'the second founder of the Order'" (MOORMAN, p. 154).

By this, far more than by a vain conformity, an exterior imitation, he is a Christ.

The man who would run after ruffians that he might make disciples of them could be pitiless toward his fellow-laborers who by an indiscreet, however well-intentioned, zeal forgot their vocation and would transform their order into a scientific institute. Can you imagine Jesus joining the school of the rabbis under the pretext of learning how to reply to them, weakening his thought by their dialectic subtleties and fantastic exegesis? He might have become a great doctor, but would he have become the Savior of the world? Probably not.

When we hear preachers going into raptures over the marvelous spread of the gospel preached by twelve poor fishermen of Galilee, we should point out to them that the miracle is at once more and less astounding than they say. It is more, for among the twelve, several returned to the shores of their charming lake, and forgetful of the mystic net, thought of the Crucified One, if they thought of him at all, only to lament him and not to raise him from the dead by continuing his work in the four quarters of the world. It is less, for if even now preachers would go forth with love, sacrificing themselves for each and all as in the old days their Master did, the miracle would be repeated again. But no; theology has killed religion.

Never was learning more eagerly coveted than in the thirteenth century. The Empire and the Church were anxiously asking of it the arguments with which they might defend their opposing claims. Innocent III sent the collection of his decretals to the University of Bologna and heaped favor upon it. Frederick II founded the school in Naples and the Patarini themselves sent their sons from Tuscany and Lombardy to study in Paris.

At the time of Francis's successful preaching in Bologna in August, 1220 (see chap. 16, pp. 107–108), he had also strongly reprimanded Peter Staccia, the provincial minister and a doctor of laws, not only for having installed the Brothers in a house that appeared to belong to them, but especially for having organized a sort of college there. It appears that the minister paid no attention to these reproaches. When Francis became aware of his obstinacy he cursed him with frightful vehemence. His indignation was so great that when, later on, Peter Staccia was about to die and his numerous friends came to beg Francis to revoke his malediction, all their efforts were in vain.

It is difficult now to imagine the rivalry that existed at this time between the Dominicans and Franciscans to draw the most illustrious masters into their respective orders. Petty intrigues were organized in which the devotees each had his part, to lead such and such a famous doctor to assume the habit. Perhaps Francis did not at the outset perceive the gravity of the danger, but illusion was no longer possible, and from this time he showed, as we have seen, an implacable firmness.

The Dominicans and the Franciscans were soon at the center of the intellectual renaissance of the thirteenth century. For example, Alexander of Hales was perhaps the most important early recruit of the Franciscans. He "was already a celebrated teacher . . . when he joined the Order of Friars Minor about the year 1236. For the next two years he ruled the newly created Franciscan school and attracted a large number of pupils. Seven years later, in August 1245, he died, leaving his Summa Theologica *. . . the first medieval writer to make use of the whole of the Aristotelian corpus"* (MOORMAN, pp. 240–41).

"Suppose," he would say, "that you had subtlety and learning enough to know all things, that you were acquainted with all languages, the courses of the stars, and all the rest— what is there to be proud of? A single demon knows more on these subjects than all the people in this world put together. But there is one thing that the demon is incapable of and that is the glory of humanity: to be faithful to God."

After the Rule of 1223 was written and approved on November 25 of that year, further demonstrating the struggles of Francis against the ministers for the preservation of his ideal, Francis and many of his companions journeyed to Rome, accepting the hospitality of Cardinal Ugolino. One day, Ugolino, and most of his guests, were surprised to find Francis absent as they were about to sit down at table. Francis soon returned, carrying a quantity of pieces of dry bread that he joyfully distributed to all the noble company. His host, somewhat abashed by this proceeding, reproached Francis a little after the meal. Francis explained that he had no right to forget, for a sumptuous feast, the bread of charity on which he was fed every day, and that he desired to show his brothers that the richest table is not worth so much to the poor in spirit as the table of the Lord.

We have seen that during the earlier years the Brothers Minor had been in the habit of earning their bread by going out as servants. Some of them—a very small number—had continued to do so. But little by little, all had changed in this matter as well. Under pretense of serving, most of the friars entered the families of the highest personages of the pontifical court and became their confidential attendants. Instead of submitting themselves to all, as the Rule of 1221 ordained, they were above everyone. By way of protest, Francis only had one weapon, his example.

It was now mid-December. An ardent desire to observe to the life and memories of Christmas had taken possession of Francis. In spite of cold and the north wind he joyfully traveled to the valley of Rieti where he opened his heart to one of his friends, the knight Giovanni of Velita, who undertook the necessary preparations.

In the Middle Ages a religious festival was above all things a representation, more or less faithful, of the event that it recalled. Hence there were the *santons* of Provence, the processions of the *Palmesel*, the Holy Supper of Maundy Thursday, the Road to the Cross of Good Friday, and the drama of the Resurrection of Easter. Francis was too thoroughly Italian not to love these festivals where every visible thing speaks of God and of God's love. The population of Greccio and its environs was, therefore, assembled, as well as the brothers from the neighboring monasteries.

santons: *Clay figurines, both secular and religious. Santons likely derive their use from the Provencal word santoun, "little saint," and are often used in manager scenes.*

Palmesel: *German carved wooden sculptures, often processed on wheels, to commemorate Christ's entry into Jerusalem riding a donkey (Mt. 21:1–11).*

Thomas of Celano, in his first life of Francis, tells us that Francis repeatedly used the phrase "bambino from Bethlehem" when referring to Jesus. "Saying the word 'Bethlehem' in the manner of a bleating sheep, he fills his whole mouth with sound but even more with sweet affection. He seems to lick his lips whenever he uses the expressions 'Jesus' or 'babe from Bethlehem,' tasting the word on his happy palate and savoring the sweetness of the word" (ARMSTRONG, p. 256). *Also, notably, Thomas, and later Bonaventure, were the first to refer to Francis as a deacon, beginning with this scene of his singing the Gospel. This could suggest that Francis was actually ordained at some point in time.*

Jacopone (d. 1306) was not only a poet but something of an early Franciscan holy fool. In public, he was known to crawl on all fours saddled as a donkey, and to appear at solemn gatherings tarred and feathered. Some scholars doubt the attribution of Stabat Mater Dolorosa to Jacopone—it has been variously ascribed to others, including Popes Innocent III and Gregory XI. It became part of the Roman Catholic breviary in 1727. The Stabat Mater Speciosa did not, and there is more consensus on Jacopone as the author of it.

The complete Stabat Mater Speciosa has thirteen double stanzas of six lines each. Sabatier quotes stanza one, lines one to three, stanza two, lines four to six, and stanza eight, lines one to three. See opposite page for a rough, English translation of the Latin quoted by Sabatier. As Sabatier mentions, the text of Stabat Mater Speciosa stands in contrast to the Stabat Mater Dolorosa, also about Mary, which begins: Stabat Mater dolorosa juxta crucem lacrimosa dum pendebat Filius ("The grieving mother stood weeping at the cross on which her son was hanging").

On the evening of the vigil of Christmas one might have seen the faithful hastening to the hermitage by every path with torches in their hands, making the forests ring with their joyful hymns.

Everyone was rejoicing—Francis most of all. The knight had prepared a stable with straw and brought an ox and a donkey, whose breath seemed to give warmth to the poor *bambino*, numbed with cold. At the sight the saint felt tears of pity warm his face; he was no longer in Greccio, his heart was in Bethlehem.

Finally they began to chant matins, then the mass was begun, and Francis, as deacon, read the Gospel. Already, hearts were touched by the simple recital of the sacred legend in a voice so gentle and so fervent, but when he preached, his emotion soon overcame the audience. His voice had so unutterable a tenderness that they also forgot everything and were living over again the feeling of the shepherds of Judea, who in those days of old went to adore the God made man, born in a stable.

Toward the close of the thirteenth century, the author of the *Stabat Mater Dolorosa*, Jacopone da Todi, that Franciscan of genius who spent a part of his life in dungeons, inspired by the memory of Greccio, composed another *Stabat*, that of joy, *Stabat Mater Speciosa*. This hymn of Mary beside the manger is not less noble than that of Mary at the foot of the cross. The sentiment is even more tender, and it is hard to explain its neglect except by an unjust caprice of fate.

Stabat Mater speciosa
Juxta foenum gaudiosa
Dum jacebat parvulus

Quae gaudebat et ridebat
Exultabat cum videbat
Nati partum inclyti

Fac me vere congaudere
Jesulino cohaerere
Donec ego vixero

The beautiful mother / stood blissfully at the crib / in which her child lay. / Joyful and laughing / and exultant she watched / the birth of her divine son. / Help me to rejoice with you / and share in the adoration of Jesus / as long as I live.

CHAPTER NINETEEN
The Stigmata (1224)

The upper valley of the Arno forms in the very center of Italy a country apart—the Casentino—which through centuries had its own life, somewhat like an island in the midst of the ocean. The river flows out from it by a narrow defile at the south, and on all other sides the Apennines encircle it with a girdle of inaccessible mountains.

The people are charming and refined; the mountains have sheltered them from wars, and on every side we see the signs of labor, prosperity, a gentle gaiety. The vegetation on the borders of the Arno is thoroughly tropical; the olive and the mulberry marry with the vine. On the lower hill-slopes are wheat fields divided by meadows, and then come the chestnuts and the oaks, higher still the pine, fir, larch, and above all the bare rock.

Among all the peaks there is one that especially attracts the attention. Instead of a rounded and somewhat flattened top, it rises slender, proud, and isolated. It is the Verna.

One might think it to be an immense rock fallen from the sky, a little like a petrified Noah's ark on the summit of Mount Ararat. The basaltic mass, perpendicular on all sides, is crowned with a plateau planted with pines and gigantic beeches, and accessible only by a footpath. Such was the solitude that Orlando, Count of Chiusi, had given to Francis, and to which Francis had already many a time come for quiet and contemplation.

La Verna is located in the Casentine Valley, south of Bologna and east of Florence. Sabatier notes that "The forest has been preserved as a relic. Alexander IV fulminated excommunication against whoever should cut down the firs of Verna" (SABATIER, p. 289). Another historian, echoing Sabatier, writes: "Its summit, covered with fir-trees, straight and close together, appears like a great whale that has rested there since the days of the flood. Below the forest lie huge boulders of rock and yawning chasms, upheaved, says the legend, during the earthquake at the time of the Crucifixion. To this solitary place came Francis in the year 1224 to celebrate by forty days of fasting and prayer the feast of St. Michael the Archangel" (GORDON, p. 72).

A monastery sits today at the top of La Verna, and in the chapel there are the famous terracotta panels (ceramics) of biblical scenes executed by members of the talented della Robbia family in the fifteenth and early sixteenth centuries. It is a popular place of pilgrimage today.

Seated upon the few stones of the Penna, the highest point on the plateau, he heard only the whispering of the wind among the trees, but in the splendor of the sunrise or the sunset he could see nearly all of the districts in which he had sown the seed of the gospel: the Romagna and the March of Ancona, losing themselves on the horizon in the waves of the Adriatic; Umbria; and farther away, Tuscany, vanishing in the waters of the Mediterranean.

Francis desired to return to La Verna after the chapter of 1224. This meeting was the last at which he was present. A new Rule was put into the hands of the ministers there, and a mission to England decided upon.

In the early days of August, Francis made his way toward La Verna. With him were only a few brothers: Masseo, Angelo, and Leo. The first had been charged to direct the little band and to spare Francis all duties except prayer.

They were on the road two days when it became necessary to seek a donkey for Francis, who was too feeble to continue on foot. The brothers, in asking for this gift, failed to conceal the name of their master, and the peasant, to whom they had addressed themselves respectfully, asked permission to join them, guiding the beast himself.

After going on for a time, the peasant said, "Is it true, that you are Brother Francis of Assisi?"

"They came to this mountain in high spirits. Francesco had accepted Count Orlando's offer without his usual reservations about the hospitality of the wealthy and powerful. The wise count had not offered them a seat at his table, soft beds, or polished floors; he did not seek, as so many did, to make house pets of the friars. Rather, he offered them a rugged wilderness in which to pray and fast, a place uninhabited because inhospitable. Francesco was convinced the invitation was from God" (MARTIN, pp. 66–67).

"Very well," he went on, after the answer was in the affirmative, "apply yourself to be as good as folk say you are, that they may not be deceived in their expectations—that is my advice."

Francis immediately got down from the donkey and, prostrating himself before the peasant, thanked him warmly.

Meanwhile, the warmest hour of the day had come on. The peasant, exhausted with fatigue, little by little forgot his surprise and joy. One does not feel the burning of thirst any less when walking beside a saint. He had begun to regret his kindness, and at that moment Francis pointed with his finger to a spring, unknown until then, and which has never been seen since.

At last they arrived at the foot of the last precipice. Before scaling it they paused to rest a little under a great oak, and immediately flocks of birds gathered around them, testifying their joy by songs and flutterings of their wings. Hovering around Francis, they alighted on his head, his shoulders, or his arms. "I see," he said joyfully to his companions, "that it is pleasing to our Lord Jesus that we live in this solitary mount, since our brothers and sisters the birds have shown such great delight at our coming."

Two of the finest paintings in the Assisi cycle of Giotto are inspired by this time on La Verna. "The Stigmata" is one of the most imitated images in the history of art, and the "Miracle of the Spring" portrays Francis in prayer to God for water on behalf of the poor peasant, and as a result, water gushing forth from dry rock. Thus was Francis shown to be a new Moses, to whom Jesus too was often compared in early Christian literature.

This mountain was at once his Tabor and his Calvary. We must not wonder, then, that legends have flourished here even more numerously than at any other period of his life. Many of them have the exquisite charm of the little flowers, rosy and perfumed, that hide themselves modestly at the feet of the fir trees of La Verna.

The summer nights up there are of unparalleled beauty. Nature, stifled by the heat of the sun, seems then to breathe anew. In the trees, behind the rocks, on the turf, a thousand voices rise up, sweetly harmonizing with the murmur of the great woods. But among all these voices there is not one that forces itself upon the attention; it is a melody that you enjoy without listening. You let your eyes wander over the landscape, still for long hours illumined with hieratic tints by the departed star of the day, and the peaks of the Apennines, flooded with rainbow hues, drop down into your soul what the Franciscan poet Thomas of Celano called the nostalgia of the everlasting hills.

More than anyone else, Francis felt it. The very evening of their arrival, seated upon a mound in the midst of his brothers, he gave them his directions for their dwelling-place. He spoke with them of his approaching death with the regret of the laborer overtaken by the shades of evening before the completion of his task, with the sighs of the father who trembles for the future of his children.

For himself during this time he desired to prepare for death by prayer and contemplation, and he begged them to protect him from all intrusion. Orlando, who had already come to bid them welcome and offer his services, had at Francis's request hastily caused a hut of boughs to be made at the foot of a great beech. It was there that Francis desired to dwell, at a stone's throw from the cells inhabited by his companions. Brother Leo was charged to bring him that which he would need each day.

In his brief "Rule for Hermitages," about five years earlier, Francis had written: "Let those who wish to stay in hermitages in a religious way be three brothers or, at the most, four; let two of these be 'the mother' and have two 'sons' or at least one. Let the two who are 'mothers' keep the life of Martha and the two 'sons' the life of Mary and let one have one enclosure in which each one may have his cell in which he may pray and sleep" (ARMSTRONG, p. 61).

He retired to his hut immediately after this memorable conversation, but several days later, embarrassed no doubt by the pious curiosity of the friars who watched all his movements, he went farther into the woods, and on Assumption Day he began there the Lent that he desired to observe.

Genius has its modesty as well as love. The poet, the artist, the saint, need to be alone when the Spirit comes to move them. Every effort of thought, of imagination, or of will is a prayer, and one does not pray in public. Jesus felt it deeply: The raptures of Tabor are brief; they may not be told.

Before these soul mysteries materialists and devotees often demand precision in the things that can the least endure it. The believer asks in what spot on the Verna Francis received the stigmata; whether the seraph that appeared to him was Jesus of a celestial spirit; what words were spoken as he imprinted them upon him; and the believer no more understands that hour when Francis fainted with woe and love than the materialist who asks to see with his eyes and touch with his hands the gaping wound.

Francis was distressed for the future of the Order, and with an infinite desire for new spiritual progress. He was consumed with the fever of saints—that need of immolation that wrung from St. Teresa the passionate cry, "Either to suffer or to die!" He was bitterly reproaching himself for not having been found worthy of martyrdom, not having been able to give himself for him who gave himself for us.

We touch here upon one of the most powerful and mysterious elements of the Christian life. We may very easily not understand it, but we may not deny it. It is the root of true mysticism. The really new thing that Jesus brought into the world was that, feeling himself in perfect union with the heavenly Father, he called all people to unite themselves to him and through him to God: "I am the vine, you are the branches. Those who abide in me and I in them bear much fruit, because apart from me you can do nothing" (Jn. 15:5).

The Christ not only preached this union, he made it felt. On the evening of his last day he instituted its sacrament, and there is probably no sect that denies that communion is at once the symbol, the principle, and the aim and goal of the religious life.

The night before he died he took the bread and broke it and distributed it to them, saying, "Take and eat, for this is my body."

Jesus, while presenting union with himself as the very foundation of the new life, took care to point out to his brethren that this union was before all things a sharing in his work, in his struggles, and his sufferings: "If any want to become my followers, let them deny themselves and take up their cross daily and follow me" (Lk. 9:23).

St. Paul entered so perfectly into the Master's thought in this respect that he uttered a few years later this cry of a mysticism that has never been equalled: "I have been crucified with Christ; and it is no longer I who live, but it is Christ who lives in me" (Gal. 2:19–20). This utterance is not an isolated exclamation with him; it is the very center of his religious consciousness. Paul goes so far as to say—at the risk of scandalizing many Christians—"In my flesh I am completing what is lacking in Christ's afflictions for the sake of his body, that is, the church" (Col. 1:24).

Perhaps it has been useful to enter into these thoughts in order to show to what point Francis is allied to the apostolic tradition during these last years of his life, as he renews in his body the passion of Christ. In the solitudes of the Verna, as formerly at San

Damiano, Jesus presented himself to him as the Crucified One, the man of sorrows.

On the Verna, Francis was even more absorbed than usual in his ardent desire to suffer for Jesus and with him. His days were divided between exercises of piety in the humble sanctuary on the mountain top and meditation in the depths of the forest. He even forgot the services, and remained several days alone in a cave of the rock going over in his heart the memories of Golgotha. At other times he would remain for long hours at the foot of the altar, reading and re-reading the Gospel and entreating God to show him the way in which he ought to walk. The book almost always opened of itself to the story of the Passion, and this simple coincidence—though easy enough to explain—was enough to excite him.

The vision of the Crucified One took fuller possession of his faculties as the day of the Elevation of the Holy Cross drew near (September 14), a festival now relegated to the background, but in the thirteenth century celebrated with a fervor and zeal very natural for a solemnity that might be considered the patronal festival of the Crusades.

Francis doubled his fastings and prayers, "quite transformed into Jesus by love and compassion," says one of the legends. He passed the night before the festival alone in prayer, not far from the hermitage. In the morning he had a vision. In the rays of the rising sun, which after the chill of night came to revive his body, he suddenly perceived a strange form. A seraph, with outspread wings, flew toward him from the edge of the horizon and bathed his soul in raptures unutterable. In the center of the vision appeared a cross, and the seraph was nailed upon it.

When the vision disappeared, he felt sharp sufferings mingling with

The story of the stigmata is told in the tales of The Little Flowers. *One historian writes that, in contrast to it, Thomas of Celano's telling of the events are "suspiciously elaborate." Sabatier follows* The Little Flowers *version more closely than the even more fantastical language of Thomas of Celano and the other early biographers. "By contrast Leo and Angelo were only a few hundred yards away and later the same morning heard from Francis's own lips what he had seen and felt.... Long after Francis died, [Brother Leo] told the full story...to a spiritual lay brother in the next generation, James of Massa. He in turn passed it on to the friars in the Marches from whom* The Little Flowers *emanated in the fourteenth century"* (HOUSE, pp. 257–58).

the ecstasy of the first moments. Stirred to the very depths of his being, he was anxiously seeking the meaning of it all when he perceived on his body the stigmata of the Crucified One.

CHAPTER TWENTY

The Canticle of the Sun
(Autumn 1224–Autumn 1225)

A little more than two weeks later, Francis left La Verna and went to Portiuncula. He was too exhausted to think of making the journey on foot, and Count Orlando put a horse at his disposal.

We can imagine the emotion with which he said goodbye to the mountain on which had been unfolded the drama of love and pain that consummated the union of his entire being with the Crucified One. If we are to believe a recently published document, Brother Masseo, one of those who remained on the Verna, made a written account of the events of this day.

They set out early in the morning. Francis, after having given his directions to the brothers, had a look and a word for everything around—for the rocks, the flowers, the trees, and for brother hawk, a privileged character that was authorized to enter his cell at all times, and that came every morning with the first glimmer of dawn to remind him of the hour of service.

Then the little band set upon the path leading to Monte-Acuto. Arriving at the gap from where one receives the last sight of the Verna, Francis alighted from his horse and, kneeling on the earth with face turned toward the mountain, said, "Adieu, mountain of God, sacred mountain, *mons coagulatus, mons pinguis, mons in quo bene placitum est Deo habitare.* Adieu, Monte-Verna, may God bless you, the Father, the Son, and the Holy Spirit. Abide in peace; we shall never see one another again."

Suddenly the Italian does not suffice and Francis is obliged to resort to the mystical language of the breviary to express his feelings. A few minutes later the rock of the ecstasy had disappeared.

"mons coagulatus, mons pinguis, mons in quo bene placitum est Deo habitare": Francis is quoting from the Latin psalter, roughly translated into English as: "a fat mountain, a curdled mountain, a mountain in which God is pleased to dwell." Even when we ascend the hill of the Lord, we can never fully penetrate the incomprehensible mysteries there. "Fat" and "curdled" are God's mysteries. (Cross-reference to Psalm 68:15–16 in today's English language psalters.)

The brothers had decided to spend the night at Monte-Casale, the little hermitage above Borgo San-Sepolcro. All of them, even those who were to remain on the Verna, were still following their master. As for Francis, he was so absorbed in thought that he became entirely oblivious to what was going on, and did not even perceive the noisy enthusiasm that his passage aroused in the numerous villages along the Tiber.

At Borgo San-Sepolcro he received a real ovation without even then coming to himself. But when they had left the town he seemed suddenly to awake and asked his companions if they would soon be arriving.

The first evening at Monte-Casale was marked by a miracle. Francis healed a friar who was possessed. The next morning, having decided to spend several days in this hermitage, Francis sent the brothers back to the Verna, and with them Count Orlando's horse.

In one of the villages through which they had passed the day before, a woman had been lying several days between death and life unable to give birth to her child. Those about her had learned of the passage of the saint through their village only when he was too far distant to be overtaken. We can imagine the joy of these poor people when the rumor was spread that he was about to return. They went to meet him and were terribly disappointed to find only the friars. Suddenly an idea occurred to them: Taking the bridle of the horse consecrated by the touch of Francis's hand, they carried it to the sufferer, who, having laid it upon her body, gave birth to her child without the slightest pain.

This miracle, established by entirely authentic narratives, shows the degree of enthusiasm felt by the people for the person of Francis. As for him, after a few days at Monte-Casale, he set out with Brother Leo for Citta of Castello. There, he healed a woman suffering from frightful nervous disorders and remained an entire month preaching in this city and its environs.

Winter was almost closing on the day when Francis and Leo finally set forth. A peasant lent Francis his donkey, but the roads were so bad that they were unable to reach any sort of shelter before nightfall. The unhappy travelers were obliged to spend the night under a rock. The shelter was more than rudimentary; the wind drifted the snow in upon them and nearly froze the unlucky peasant who, with abominable oaths, heaped curses on Francis. But Francis replied with such cheerfulness that he made the peasant at last forget both the cold and his bad humor.

The next day, the saint reached Portiuncula. He stayed only briefly, however, and soon left to evangelize southern Umbria. We know almost nothing of this trip, except that Brother Elias accompanied him, and Francis was so feeble that Elias could not conceal his uneasiness about it. Ever since his return from Syria (August 1220), Francis had been growing continually weaker, but his fervor had increased from day to day. Nothing could check him, neither suffering nor the entreaties of the brothers. Seated on a donkey he would sometimes travel to three or four villages in one day. But now he was losing his sight.

Meanwhile a sedition had forced Honorius III to leave Rome (end of April 1225). After passing a few weeks at Tivoli, he established himself at Rieti, where he remained until the end of 1226. The pope's arrival had drawn to this city, with the entire pontifical court, several physicians of renown. Cardinal Ugolino, who had come in the pope's train, hearing of Francis's malady, summoned him to Rieti for treatment. But despite Brother Elias's urging, Francis hesitated a long time before accepting the invitation. It seemed to him that a sick man has but one thing to do—place himself purely and simply in the hands of the heavenly Father. What is pain to a soul that is fixed in God!

Elias, however, overcame his objections at last and the journey was determined, but first Francis desired to go and see Clare and enjoy a little rest near her. He remained at San Damiano much longer than he had proposed to do, from the end of July to the beginning of September 1225. His arrival at this beloved monastery was marked by a terrible aggravation of his malady. For fifteen days he was so completely blind that he could not even distinguish light. The care lavished on him produced no result, since every day he passed long hours in weeping—tears of penitence, he said, but also of regret. How different they were from those tears of his moments of inspiration and emotion that had flowed over a countenance all illumined with joy! They had seen him, in such moments, take up two bits of wood, and, accompanying himself with this rustic violin, improvise French songs in which he would pour out the abundance of his heart.

But the radiance of genius and hope had now become dimmed. Rachel weeps for her children and will not be comforted because they are not. There are in the tears of Francis this same *quia non sunt* for his spiritual sons.

"Ah, if the brothers knew what I suffer," St. Francis said a few days before the impression of the stigmata, "with what pity and compassion they would be moved!" But they, seeing in him the one who had laid cheerfulness upon them as a duty becoming more and more sad and keeping aloof from them, imagined that he was tortured with temptations of the devil.

Clare divined what could not be uttered. At San Damiano her friend was looking back over all the past. Here, the olive-tree to which, a brilliant cavalier, he had fastened his horse; there, the stone bench where his friend, the priest of the poor chapel, used to sit; over there, the hiding-place in which he had taken refuge from the paternal wrath; and, above all, the sanctuary with the mysterious crucifix of the decisive hour.

In living over these pictures of the radiant past, Francis aggravated his pain, yet they spoke to him of other things than death and regret. Clare was there, as steadfast, as ardent as ever. Long ago transformed by admiration, she was now transfigured by compassion. Seated at the feet of him whom she loved with more than earthly love she felt the soreness of his soul, and the failing of his heart.

She kept him near her, and taking part in the labor, she made him a large cell of reeds in the monastery garden, so that he might

In the nave of the Upper Basilica di San Francesco in Assisi are twenty-eight frescos representing the life and legend of Francis. The great painter Giotto is believed to be their creator, although this is hotly debated even today. At this point in our narrative of Francis's life, we have just passed number nineteen in the cycle, that of Francis receiving the stigmata. Other scenes from these paintings are never discussed by Sabatier and most modern biographers, including a vision of some of the brothers at Rivo-Torto of Francis traveling to heaven in a chariot like Elijah (number eight), and a vision of Brother Leo in which the highest throne of heaven, formerly occupied by Satan (before the angels revolted) is reserved for Francis, the most humble (number nine).

be entirely at liberty as to his movements. How could he refuse a hospitality so thoroughly Franciscan? It was indeed, but only too much so: Legions of rats and mice infested this retired spot. At night they ran over Francis's bed with an infernal uproar, such that he could find no rest from his sufferings. But he soon forgot all of that when near his sister-friend. Once again she gave back to him faith and courage. "A single sunbeam," he used to say, "is enough to drive away many shadows."

Little by little the man of the former days began to show himself, and at times the sisters would hear, mingling with the murmur of the olive trees and pines, the echo of unfamiliar songs seeming to come from the cell of reeds. One day he was seated at the monastery table after a long conversation with Clare. The meal had hardly begun when suddenly he seemed to be rapt away in ecstasy. *"Laudato sia lo Signore!"* ("Praise the Lord!") he cried on coming to himself. He had just composed "The Canticle of the Sun."

> O most high, almighty, good Lord God,
> to you belong praise, glory, honor, and all blessing!
> Praised be my Lord God with all Your creatures,
> and especially our Brother Sun,
> who brings us the day and who brings us the light.
> Fair is he and shines with a very great splendor:
> O Lord, he signifies You to us!
> Praised be my Lord for our Brother Wind,
> and for air and cloud, calms and all weather
> through which You uphold life in all creatures.
> Praised be my Lord for our Sister Water,
> who is very useful to us and humble and precious and clean.
> Praised be my Lord for our Brother Fire,
> through whom You give us light in the darkness;
> and he is bright and pleasant and very mighty and strong.
> Praised be my Lord for our Mother Earth,
> who does sustain us and keep us,
> and brings forth many fruits and flowers of many colors, and grass.
> Praised be my Lord for all those who pardon one another for Your sake,
> and who endure weakness and tribulation;

blessed are they who peaceably endure, for You, O most High,

shall give them a crown.

Praised be my Lord for our Sister Death of the Body,

from whom no one can escape.

Woe to those who die in mortal sin.

Blessed are they who are found walking by Your most holy will,

for the second death shall have no power to do them harm.

Praise and bless the Lord, and give thanks to Him

and serve Him with great humility.

Joy had returned to Francis, joy as deep as ever. For a whole week he put aside his breviary and passed his days in repeating "The Canticle of the Sun."

During a night of sleeplessness he heard a voice saying to him, "If you had faith as a grain of mustard seed, you would say to this mountain, 'Be removed from here,' and it would move away." Was not the mountain his sufferings, the temptation to murmur and despair? "Be it, Lord, according to your word," Francis replied with all his heart, and immediately he felt that he was delivered.

Francis might have perceived that the mountain had not greatly changed its place, but for several days he turned his eyes away from it and had been able to forget its existence.

For a moment he thought of summoning to his side Brother Pacifico, the king of verse, to retouch his canticle. His idea was to attach to him a certain number of friars who would go with him from village to

It is fairly easy to imagine how the originality of Francis's ideas was not always appreciated within the established norms of traditional religious life. This story—of Francis teaching his brothers to be God's jugglers—recalls the vehement words of the old monk, Jorge, in Umberto Eco's novel The Name of the Rose. *Jorge poisoned the pages of a hidden book about laughter in the abbey scriptorium, wanting to protect the young and the curious from the greater poison of laughter: a "weakness, corruption, the foolishness of our flesh." At the end of the novel, Jorge says with contempt to his accuser, a Franciscan: "You are a clown, like the saint who gave birth to you all. You are like your Francis, who ... begged in French, and imitated with a piece of wood the movements of a violin player, who disguised himself as a tramp to confound the gluttonous monks, who flung himself naked in the snow, spoke with animals and plants, transformed the very mystery of the Nativity into a village spectacle, called the lamb of Bethlehem by imitating the bleat of a sheep" (ECO 2, pp. 474, 477–78).*

village, preaching. After the sermon they would sing the hymn of the sun, and they were to close by saying to the gathered crowd, "We are God's jugglers. We desire to be paid for our sermon and our song. Our payment will be that you persevere in penitence."

"Is it not in fact true," Francis would add, "that the servants of God are really like jugglers, intended to revive the hearts of men and lead them into spiritual joy?"

The Francis of the old raptures was back—the layman, the poet, the artist.

CHAPTER TWENTY-ONE

His Last Year
(September 1225–End of
September 1226)

Francis's notion of friars being God's jugglers turned on their head the traditional religious attitudes toward spontaneous movement and song. Before Francis, a religious person (in particular, a monk) was supposed to be, like the angels, static in movement and grave in emotion. The Cistercian theologian Bernard of Clairvaux, a century before Francis, disparagingly compared a juggler's gyrating body with a monk's bent body in prayer: "In fact what else do seculars think we are doing but playing when what they desire most on earth, we fly from; and what they fly from we desire? Like acrobats and jugglers who with their heads down and feet up, stand or walk on their heads, and thus draw all eyes to themselves. But this is not a game for children or the theatre where lust is excited by the effeminate and indecent contortions of the actors, it is a joyous game, decent, grave and admirable, delighting the gaze of heavenly onlookers" (CAMILLE, p. 59).

What would Ugolino have thought of Francis's plan to send out his friars, transformed into God's jugglers, singing "The Canticle of Brother Sun" throughout the countryside? Perhaps he never heard of it. But his protégé finally decided to accept his invitation and left San Damiano in September 1225.

The landscape that lies before the eyes of the traveler from Assisi, when suddenly emerging on the plain of Rieti, is one of the most beautiful in Europe. From Terni the road follows the sinuous course of the Velino, passes not far from the famous cascades, whose clouds of mist are visible, and then plunges into the defiles in whose depths the torrent rushes noisily, choked by a vegetation as luxuriant as that of a virgin forest. On all sides are walls of perpendicular rocks, and on their crests, several hundred yards above your head, are feudal fortresses, among others the Castle of Miranda.

After four hours of walking, you see the defile opening out and you find yourself without transition in a broad valley, sparkling with light. The highway goes directly toward Rieti, passing between tiny lakes; here and there roads lead off to little villages, which you see, on the hillsides, between the cultivated fields and the edge of the forests; there are Stroncone, Greccio, Cantalice, Poggio-Buscone, and ten other small towns that have given more saints to the Church than a whole province of France.

Francis had often gone over this district in every direction. Like its neighbor, the hilly March of Ancona, it was peculiarly prepared to receive the new gospel. In these hermitages, with their almost impossible simplicity, perched near the villages on every side without the least care for material comfort, was a school of the Brothers Minor—impassioned, proud, stubborn, almost wild, who did not wholly understand their master, who did not catch his exquisite simplicity, his dreams of social and political renovation, his poetry and delicacy, but who did understand the lover of nature and of poverty. They did more than understand him; they lived his life, and from that Christmas festival observed in the woods of Greccio down to today they have remained the simple and popular representatives of the Strict Observance. From them comes *The Legend of the Three Companions*, the most lifelike and true of all the portraits of the Poverello, and it was there, in a cell three paces long, that Giovanni of Parma had his apocalyptic visions.

The news of Francis's arrival spread quickly, and long before he reached Rieti the population had come out to meet him. To avoid this noisy welcome, he craved the hospitality of the priest of St. Fabian. This little chapel, now known under the name of Our Lady of the Forest, stands somewhat aside from the road on a grassy mound about three miles from the city. He was heartily welcomed there, and as he desired to remain for a little, prelates and devotees began to flock there over the following few days.

It was the time of the early grapes. It is easy to imagine the disquietude of the priest on perceiving the ravages made by these visitors among his vines, his best source of revenue, but he probably exaggerated the damage. One day, Francis heard him venting about his misfortune.

"Father," Francis said, "it is useless for you to disturb yourself for what you cannot control. But, tell me, how much wine do you get on average?"

"Fourteen measures," replied the priest.

"Very well, if you have less than twenty this year, I will make up the difference." This promise reassured the worthy man, and when at the vintage he received twenty measures, he had no hesitation in believing in a miracle.

After Ugolino's pleadings, Francis accepted the hospitality of the bishop's palace in Rieti. Thomas of Celano enlarges with delight on the marks of devotion lavished on Francis by this prince of the Church.

It is important to realize that Francis, in his own lifetime, entered into the condition of a relic. The mania for amulets displayed itself around him in all its excesses. People quarreled not only over his clothing, but even over his hair and the parings of his nails. Did these exterior demonstrations disgust him? Did he sometimes think of the contrast between these honors offered to his body, which he picturesquely called "Brother Ass," and the subversion of his ideal? If he had feelings of this kind, those who surrounded him were not the people to understand them, and it would be idle to expect any expression of them from his pen.

Pilgrims and tourists to the basilica in Assisi may see the tunic worn by St. Francis. He wrote, beautifully, in the first Rule: "Let all the brothers wear poor clothes and, with the blessing of God, they can patch them with sackcloth and other pieces.... [L]et them ... not cease doing good nor seek expensive clothing in this world, so that they may have a garment in the kingdom of heaven" (ARMSTRONG, p. 65). Francis's tunic shows signs of his loving patchwork.

Soon after arriving at the bishop's palace Francis had a relapse and asked to be moved to Monte-Colombo, a hermitage hidden amidst trees and scattered rocks an hour distant from Rieti. He knew this place, having retired there several times before, most notably while preparing the Rule of 1223.

The doctors attending him had exhausted the therapeutic arsenal of the time and decided to resort to cauterization. It was decided to draw a rod of white-hot iron across his forehead.

When the poor patient saw them bringing in the brazier and the instruments, he had a moment of terror, and immediately making the sign of the cross over the glowing iron, said, "Brother fire, you are beautiful above all creatures. Be favorable to me in this hour. You know how much I have always loved you. Be courteous, then, today."

After the crude procedure was over, and his companions who had not had the courage to remain, came back, Francis said, smiling, "Oh, cowardly folk, why did you go away? I felt no pain. Brother doctor, if it is necessary you may do it again."

This experiment was no more successful than the other remedies. In vain they revitalized the wound on the forehead by applying plasters, salves, and even by making incisions in it. The only result was to increase the pains of the sufferer.

One day in Rieti soon thereafter, Francis thought that a little music would relieve his pain. Calling a friar who had formerly been clever at playing the guitar, he begged him to borrow one; but the friar was afraid of the scandal this might cause, and so Francis gave up the idea.

But God took pity on him, and sent the following night an invisible angel to give Francis such a concert as is never heard on Earth. Hearing the music, Francis lost all bodily feeling, according to *The Little Flowers*, and at one moment the melody was so sweet and penetrating that if the angel had given one more stroke of the bow, the sick man's soul would have left his body.

Francis was attended to by papal physicians, presumably the best in the land, but in the end, all medicine before science was fairly much the same. Geoffrey Chaucer (d. 1400), in the Prologue to his Canterbury Tales, *characterizes the physician with tongue-in-cheek humor that would be generally accurate of medicine before science at the time of St. Francis:*

> With us there was a doctor of physic;
> In all this world was none like him
>   to pick
> For talk of medicine and surgery;
> For he was grounded in astronomy.
> He often kept a patient from the pall
> By horoscopes and magic natural.
> Well could he tell the fortune
>   ascendant
> Within the houses for his sick patient.
> He knew the cause of every malady,
> Were it of hot or cold, of moist or
>   dry,
> And where engendered, and of what
>   humour;
> He was a very good practitioner.
> (SOURCEBOOK, lines 411–22)

There was some degree of amelioration of his condition when the doctors left him, and we find him throughout the most remote hermitages of Umbria during the winter months of 1225 to 1226. As soon as he had gained a little strength he was determined to begin preaching again.

He went to Poggio-Buscone, a three hours' walk north from Rieti, for the Christmas festival. People flocked there in crowds from all over the country to see and hear him. "You come here," he said, expecting to find a great saint. What will you think when I tell you that I ate meat all through Advent?"

At St. Eleutheria, a few minutes walk from Rieti, at a time of extreme cold that tried Francis very much, he had sewn some pieces of stuff into his tunic, and that of his companion, in order to make their garments a little warmer. One day his companion came home with a fox-skin, with which he proposed to line his master's tunic. Francis rejoiced over this, but would permit this excess consideration for his body only on the condition that the piece of fur be placed on the outside, over his chest. Each of these incidents, almost insignificant at first view, show how he detested hypocrisy even in the smallest detail.

We will not follow him to his dear Greccio, or to the hermitage of St. Urbano, perched on one of the highest peaks of the Sabine. The accounts that we have of the brief visits he made there at this time tell us nothing new of his character or of the history of his life. They simply show that the imaginations of those who surrounded him were extraordinarily overheated; the smallest incidents immediately took on a miraculous coloring.

There are many legends about the origin of Portiuncula, the "little portion" of a place where Francis lived, and later, insisted on dying. Legend has it that fourth-century hermits from the Valley of Josaphat first built the Portiuncula chapel to house relics in their possession from the grave of the Blessed Virgin. It is also believed that in the early sixth century the chapel was occupied by St. Benedict, author of the well-known Rule for monks. The chapel, Santa Maria degli Angeli, or "Our Lady of the Angels," most likely gained its name as a reference to the legend of Mary's ascent into heaven in the company of angels. Other local legends attribute the name of Francis's beloved little place to the occasional singing of angels actually heard there.

The documents also do not say how it came about that Francis decided to go to Siena. Apparently, there was in that city a physician of great fame as an occultist. The treatment he prescribed was no more successful than that of the others, but with the return of spring Francis made a new effort to return to active life. We find him describing the ideal Franciscan monastery, and another day explaining a passage in the Bible to a Dominican.

Did the latter, a doctor of theology, desire to ridicule the rival order by showing its founder incapable of explaining a some-what difficult verse? It appears extremely likely.

"My good father," he said, "how do you understand this say-ing of the prophet Ezekiel, 'If you do not warn the wicked of his wickedness, I will require his soul of you'? I am acquainted with many people whom I know to be in a state of moral sin, and yet I am not always reproaching them for their vices. Am I, then, responsible for their souls?"

At first Francis excused himself, alleging his ignorance, but urged by his interlocutor he said at last: "Yes, the true servant unceas-ingly rebukes the wicked, but he does it most of all by his conduct, by the truth that shines in his words, by the light of his example, by all the radiance of his life."

He soon suffered a relapse so grave that the brothers thought his last hour had come. They were especially frightened by the hemorrhages, which reduced him to complete prostration. Brother Elias hurried to his side and at his arrival acquiesced to Francis's desire to be taken back to Umbria. Toward the middle of April they set out, going in the direction of Cortona. It is the easiest route, and at the delightful hermitage of that city Francis remained for a short time. But Francis was in a hurry to see once more the skies of his native country, Portiuncula, San Damiano, the Carceri, all those paths and hamlets that one sees from the terraces of Assisi and that recalled in him so many sweet memories.

Instead of going by the nearest road, they made a long circuit by Gubbio and Nocera, to avoid Perugia, fearing some attempt of the people there to take possession of the saint. Such a relic as the body of Francis held a value similar to that of the sacred nails of the true cross or the sacred lance of Christ's passion. Battles were fought over less than that.

They made a short stop near Nocera, about an hour east at the her-mitage of Bagnara, on the slopes of Monte-Pennino. His companions

"Two years after Francis's death, the King of France and all his court kissed and revered the pillow that Francis had used during his illness" (SABATIER, p. 315).

were again very worried. The swelling that was showing itself in Francis's lower limbs was rapidly gaining in the upper part of his body, as well. The Assisans learned this, and wishing to be prepared for whatever might happen, sent their men-at-arms to protect the saint and to hasten his return.

Bringing Francis back with them, the brothers and soldiers stopped for food at the hamlet of Balciano, about halfway between Nocera and Assisi. In vain they begged the inhabitants to sell them provisions. As the escorts were confiding their disappointment to the friars, Francis, who knew these good peasants, said: "If you had asked for food without offering to pay, you would have found all that you wanted." He was right, for, following his advice, the men received all that they desired, for nothing.

The arrival of the party at Assisi was hailed with frantic joy. This time Francis's fellow-citizens were sure that the saint was not going to die somewhere else. Thomas of Celano, in fact, is even more explicit: "The multitude hoped that he would die very soon, and that was the subject of their joy."

The customs of relics and their importance have changed so much that we cannot thoroughly comprehend the good fortune of possessing the body of a saint. We find here several incidents that we may be tempted to consider shocking or even ignoble, if we do not make an effort to put them all into their proper surroundings.

Francis was installed in the bishop's palace; he would have preferred to be at Portiuncula, but the brothers were obliged to obey the injunctions of the populace, and to

Saints' relics were indeed highly prized in the late Middle Ages. "Although major liturgical manuals of the twelfth and thirteenth centuries insisted that it is logically impossible for one body to be buried in two places, this is exactly what happened. The bodies of the saints were divided up to provide relics. Division of the saints resulted not merely (as it had in antiquity) from the kinds of execution martyrs suffered at the hands of their tormentors. . . . Division was now also deliberately practiced immediately after death. Holy bodies were cut up so that parts could be given to religious communities that wished to share in the saint's power and presence. . . . When monks and canons squabbled over the relics of saints or the entrails of kings and cardinals, they were fighting for possession of more than the revenues associated with masses for the dead. The greater the number of parts and places in which noble or holy figures rested after death, the more far-flung their presence" (BYNUM, pp. 201–2, 205). The relics of saints were housed in containers called reliquaries, beautiful vessels of different shapes and designs often decorated with elaborate jewels and gold plating.

make doubly sure that it was safe, with guards placed at all the entrances to the palace. Francis remained much longer here than anyone had anticipated; it perhaps lasted several months (July to September). This dying man did not want yet to die. His anxieties for the future of the Order, which a little while before had been in the background, now returned, more agonizing and terrible than ever.

"We must begin again," he thought, "and create a new family who will not forget humility, who will go and serve lepers and, as in the old times, put themselves always, not merely in words, but in reality, below all men." To be obliged to look on at the dreaded decomposition of his order, he, the lark, to be spied upon by soldiers watching for his corpse—there was quite enough here to make Francis mortally sad.

Four Brothers had been especially charged to lavish care upon him: Leo, Angelo, Rufino, and Masseo. We already know them; they are of those intimate friends of the first days who had heard in the Franciscan gospel a call to love and liberty.

One day one of them said to the sick man: "Father, you are going away to leave us here. Point out to us, then, if you know him, the one to whom we might in all security confide the burden of the generalship of the Order."

Francis did not know the ideal brother who was capable of assuming such a duty, but he took advantage of the question to sketch the portrait of the perfect minister general We have two versions of this portrait, the one that was retouched by Thomas of Celano, and the original, much shorter and more vague, but showing us Francis desiring that his successors should have but a single weapon, an unalterable love. And so he left his successors, the ministers general of the Order, a letter that they should pass on from one to another, and where they should find, not directions for particular situations, but the very inspiration of their activity.

> To the Reverend Father in Christ, Minister General of the entire Order of the Brothers Minor. May God bless you and keep you in his holy love.
>
> Patience in all things and everywhere, this, my brother, is what I especially recommend. Even if they oppose you, if they strike you, you should be grateful to them and desire that it should be thus and not otherwise.

In this will be manifest your love for God and for me, his servant and yours, that there shall not be a single friar in the world who, having sinned as much as one can sin, and coming before you, shall go away without having received your pardon. And if he does not ask it, you ask it for him, whether he wills it or not.

And if he should return again a thousand times before you, love him more than myself in order to lead him to doing well. Have pity always on these brothers.

These words show plainly how Francis had directed the Order in former days. In his dream the ministers general were to act with pure affection and tender devotion toward those under them. But was this possible for one at the head of a family whose branches extended over the entire world? It would be hazardous to say, for his successors have not been wanting for distinguished minds and noble hearts, but with the exception of Giovanni of Parma and two or three others, this ideal is in sharp contrast with the reality. St. Bonaventure himself would later drag his master and friend, Giovanni of Parma, before an ecclesiastical tribunal, causing him to be condemned to perpetual imprisonment. Only the intervention of a cardinal outside of the Order finally secured the commutation of the sentence.

The agonies of grief endured by the dying Francis over the decadence of the Order would have been less poignant if they had not been mingled with self-reproaches for his own cowardice. Why had he deserted his post, given up the direction of his family, if not from idleness and selfishness? And now it was too late to take back this step; in hours of frightful anguish he asked himself if God would hold him responsible for this subversion of the ideal.

Shattered by fever, Francis would suddenly rise up in his bed, crying with a despairing intensity: "Where are they who have ravished my brothers from me? Where are they who have stolen away my family?"

Alas, the real criminals were nearer to him than he thought. The provincial ministers, of whom he appears to have been thinking when he spoke those words, were only instruments in the hands of the clever Brother Elias, and what else was he doing but putting his intelligence and energy at Cardinal Ugolino's service?

Far from finding any consolation in those around him, Francis was constantly tortured by the confidences of his companions, who, compelled by mistaken zeal, aggravated his pain instead of calming it. Witness this exchange, supposed to have been between Brother Leo and his spiritual father:

"Forgive me, Father," said one of them to him one day, "but many people have already thought what I am going to say to you. You know how, in the early days, by God's grace the Order walked in the path of perfection? All that concerns poverty and love, as well as for all the rest, the brothers were of one heart and one soul. But for some time now that is entirely changed. It is true that people often excuse the brothers by saying that the Order has grown too large to keep up the old observances. They even go so far as to claim that infidelities to the Rule, such as the building of great monasteries, are a means of edification of the people, and so the primitive simplicity and poverty are held for nothing. Evidently, all of these abuses are displeasing to you. But then, people ask, why do you tolerate them?"

"God forgive you, brother," replied Francis. "Why do you lay at my door things I can do nothing about? As long as I had direction of the Order, and the brothers persevered in their vocation, I was able in spite of weakness to do what was needed. But when I saw that, without caring for my example or my teaching, they walked in the ways you have described, I confided them to the Lord and to the ministers. It is true that when I relinquished the direction of the Order, alleging my incapacity as the motive, if they had walked in the way of my wishes I would have desired that until my death they would never have another minister."

Francis's complaints became so sharp and bitter that, to avoid scandal, the greatest prudence was exercised as to who was permitted to see him. Disorder was everywhere, and every day brought with it a new contingent of subjects for sorrow. There was much confusion of how to practice the Rule—the Franciscan ideal was veiled, not only from brothers in faraway places, or those who had recently joined the Order, but even from those who had lived under the influence of the founder. Under these circumstances, Francis dictated a letter to all members of the Order, which he thought would be read at the opening of chapters and perpetuate his spiritual presence among them.

In the letter Francis is perfectly true to himself. As in the past, he desires to influence the brothers not by reproaches but by fixing their eyes on perfect holiness.

> To all the revered and beloved Brothers Minor, to Brother A_____ [here the future copyists were to insert the name of the current minister general], minister general, its Lord, and to the ministers-general who shall come after him, and to all the ministers, custodians, and priests of this fraternity, humble in Christ, and to all the simple and obedient brothers, the oldest and the most recent, Brother Francis, a small and dying man, your little servant, gives you greeting!
>
> Hear, my lords, you who are my sons and my brothers, give ear to my words. Open your hearts and obey the voice of the Son of God. Keep his commandments with all your hearts and perfectly observe his counsels. Praise him for he is good, and glorify him by your works.
>
> God has sent you through all the world that by your words and example you may bear witness of him, and so that you may teach all people that he alone is all powerful. Persevere in discipline and obedience, and with an honest and firm will keep what you have promised.

After this opening, Francis immediately moves to the essential matter of the letter: the love and respect due to the sacrament of the altar. Faith in this mystery of love appeared to Francis to be equivalent with the very salvation of the Order. To Francis, the question of this dogma presented itself quite differently than it does to most of us today for whom faith belongs solely in the intellectual sphere. The thought that there could be any merit in believing never entered his mind; the fact of the real presence of God in the host was for him of almost concrete evidence. Therefore his faith in this mystery was an energy of the heart—that the life of God, mysteriously present upon the altar, might become the soul of all his actions.

To the eucharistic transubstantiation, effected by the words of the priest, Francis added another, that of his own heart:

> God offers himself to us as to his children. This is why I beg you, all of you, my brothers, kissing your feet, and with all the love of which I am capable, to have all possible respect for the body and blood of our Lord Jesus Christ.

Then, addressing himself particularly to the priests:

If the blessed Virgin Mary is justly honored for having carried Jesus in her womb, if John the Baptist trembled because he dared not touch the Lord's head, if the sepulcher in which he lay for a little time is regarded with such adoration, oh, how holy, pure, and worthy should be the priest who touches with his hands, who receives into his mouth and into his heart, and who distributes to others the living, glorified Jesus, the sight of whom makes angels rejoice!

Understand your dignity, brother priests, and be holy, for he is holy. Let each man be struck with amazement, let the whole earth tremble, let the heavens thrill with joy when the Christ, the Son of the living God, descends upon the altar into the hands of the priest. Oh, wonderful profundity! Oh, amazing grace! Oh, triumph of humility! See, the Master of all things, God, and the Son of God, humbles himself for our salvation, even to disguising himself under the appearance of a bit of bread. Contemplate, my brothers, this humility of God and enlarge your hearts before him.

We see what vigor of love Francis's heart held for Holy Communion. He closes this section of his letter with long counsels to the brothers, and after having urged them to keep their promises faithfully, all his mysticism breathes out and is summed up in a prayer of admirable simplicity.

God Almighty, eternal, righteous, and merciful, give to us poor wretches to do for your sake all that we know of your will, and to will always what pleases you, so that inwardly purified, enlightened, and kindled by the fire of the Holy Spirit, we may follow in the footprints of your beloved Son, our Lord Jesus Christ.

Francis's solicitudes reached far beyond the limits of the Franciscan Order. His longest epistle is addressed to all Christians. Its words are so living that you might think you hear a voice speaking behind you, and this voice, almost as serene as the one from the mountain in Galilee that proclaimed the law of the new times, becomes here and there unutterably sweet, like that one that sounded in the upper chamber on the night of the first eucharist.

As Jesus forgot the cross that was standing in the shadows, so Francis forgets his sufferings and, overcome with a divine sadness, thinks of humanity, for whom he would give his life. He thinks of his spiritual sons whom he is about to leave without having been able to make them feel as he would have them feel: "Father, I have given them the words that you have given me.... For them I pray!"

The whole Franciscan gospel is in these words, but to understand the fascination that it exerted we must have gone through the school of the Middle Ages and there listened to the interminable tournaments of dialectics by which minds were dried up. We have already seen the Church of the thirteenth century, honeycombed by simony and luxury, and able, under the pressure of heresy or revolt, only to make a few futile efforts to stop the evil.

> To all Christians, monks, clerics, or laypeople, whether men or women, to all who dwell in the whole world, Brother Francis, their most submissive servant, presents his duty and wishes the true peace of heaven and sincere love in the Lord.
>
> Being the servant of all people, I am bound to serve them and to give to them the wholesome words of my Master. This is why, seeing I am too weak and ill to visit each one of you in particular, I have resolved to send you my message by this letter and to offer you the words of our Lord Jesus Christ, the Word of God, and of the Holy Spirit, which are spirit and life.

He closes by showing the foolishness of those who set their hearts on the possession of earthly goods, and concludes with a very realistic picture of the death of the wicked.

> His money, his title, his learning, all that he believed himself to possess, all are taken from him. The worms will eat his body and the demons will consume his soul, and he will lose both soul and body.
>
> I, Brother Francis, your little servant, beg and ask you by the love that is in God, ready to kiss your feet, to receive with humility and love these and all other words of our Lord Jesus Christ and to conform your conduct to them. Let those who devoutly receive them and understand them pass them on to others. And if they persevere in them unto the end, may they be blessed by the Father, the Son, and the Holy Spirit. Amen.

If Francis ever made a Rule for the Third Order it must have closely resembled this epistle. Everything in these long pages looks toward the development of the mystic religious life in the heart of each Christian. But even when Francis dictated them, this high view had become a utopia, and the Third Order was only one battalion more in the armies of the papacy.

Francis also did not forget his sister-friend at San Damiano. Hearing that she was troubled, knowing him to be so ill, he desired to reassure her. He still deceived himself as to his real condition, writing to Clare promising soon to come and see her. To this assurance he added some affectionate counsels, advising her and her companions not to go to extremes with their penances. In order to set her an example of cheerfulness he added a laud in the vernacular, which he set to music himself.

Meanwhile, the bishop of Assisi, the irritable Guido, always at war with somebody, was at this time quarrelling with the governor of the city. Nothing more was needed to excite in the little town a profound disquiet. Guido had excommunicated the governor, and the latter had issued a prohibition against selling, buying, or making any contract with ecclesiastics. The differences grew more bitter and no one appeared to dream of attempting a reconciliation. We can better understand Francis's grief over this if we remember that his very first effort had been to bring peace to his native city, and that he considered the return of Italy to union and concord to be the essential aim of his apostolate. War in Assisi would be the final dissolution of his dream.

The dregs of this cup were spared him, thanks to an inspiration that broke forth from his imagination. To the Canticle of the Sun he added a new verse:

> Be praised, Lord, for those who forgive for love of you,
> and bear trials and tribulations.
> Happy are they who persevere in peace,
> by you, Most High, shall they be crowned.

Then, calling a friar, he charged him with begging the governor to go, with all of the notable people whom he could assemble, to the paved square in front of the bishop's palace. The governor, to whom legend gives the nobler part in the whole affair, at once yielded to the saint's request. As we hear from eyewitnesses:

When he arrived and the bishop had come out of the palace, two friars stepped forward and said: "Brother Francis has made, for the praise of God, a hymn which he prays you will listen to." And immediately they began to sing the hymn of Brother Sun with its new verse.

The governor listened, standing in an attitude of profound attention, weeping, for he dearly loved the blessed Francis. When the singing ended, he said, "Know in truth that I desire to forgive the lord bishop, that I wish and ought to look on him as my lord, for if someone were even to assassinate my brother I would be ready to pardon the murderer."

With these words he threw himself at the bishop's feet and said, "I am ready to do whatever you wish, for the love of our Lord Jesus Christ and his servant Francis."

The bishop took him by the hand, lifted him up and said, "In my position it would become me to be humble, but since I am naturally too quick to wrath, you must pardon me."

This unexpected reconciliation was immediately looked on as miraculous, increasing even more the reverence of the Assisans for their fellow-citizen.

The summer was drawing to a close. After a few days of relative improvement, Francis's sufferings became greater than ever. Incapable of movement, he even thought that he ought to give up his ardent desire to see San Damiano and Portiuncula once more, and gave the brothers all his directions about the latter sanctuary: "Never abandon it, for that place is truly sacred. It is the house of God." It seemed to him that if the brothers remained attached to that bit of earth, that chapel ten feet long, those thatched huts, they would find there the living reminder of the poverty of the early days, and could never wander far from it.

After hearing from a doctor that he was not expected to live past the autumn, Francis cried with an expression of joy, "Welcome, Sister Death!" He began to sing and sent for Brothers Angelo and Leo. When they arrived they were made, in spite of their emotion, to sing the Canticle of Brother Sun. They were at the last doxology when Francis, stopping them, improvised the greeting to death:

> Be praised, Lord, for our Sister Death of the body,
> from whom no one may escape.
> Alas for them who die in a state of mortal sin;
> happy they are who are found to have conformed to
> your most holy will,
> for the second death will do them no harm.

From this day the palace rang unceasingly with his songs. Continually, even through the night, he would sing the Canticle of Brother Sun or some others of his favorite compositions. Then, wearied, he would beg Angelo and Leo to go on.

One day Brother Elias thought it his duty to make a few remarks on the subject. He feared that the nurses and the people of the neighborhood would be scandalized; ought not a saint to be absorbed in meditation in the face of death, awaiting it with fear and trembling rather than indulging in gaiety that might be misinterpreted? Perhaps

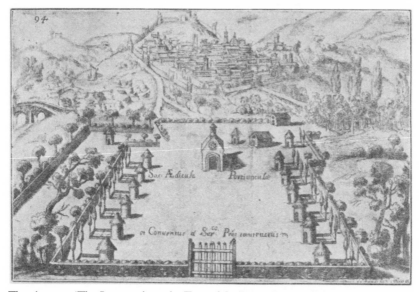

This drawing, "The Portiuncula in the Time of St. Francis," originally appeared in a book published in Montefalco, Italy, in 1704. The proximity of Portiuncula to Assisi in the background is clear, as is the original chapel, and to the right of it, the infirmary where Francis died, now called the "Chapel of St. Francis." Surely, the gate seen in this drawing (and probably quite a bit more) was added later, after Francis's death. (GORDON, p. 107)

Bishop Guido, too, was troubled. It seems likely that he was annoyed at having his palace crowded with Brothers Minor all these long weeks. But Francis would not yield; his union with God was too sweet for him to consent not to sing it.

They decided at last to move Francis to Portiuncula. His desire was to be fulfilled. He was to die beside the humble chapel where he had heard God's voice consecrating him an apostle.

His companions, bearing their precious burden, took the way through the olive-yards across the plain. From time to time the invalid, unable to distinguish anything, asked where they were. When they were halfway there, at the hospital of the Carceri where long ago he had tended the leper, and from where there was a full view of all the houses of the city, he begged them to set him on the ground with his face toward Assisi. Raising his hand he bade adieu to his native place and blessed it.

CHAPTER TWENTY-TWO
Francis's Will and Death
(End of September—October 3, 1226)

The last days of Francis's life were radiant with beauty. He went to meet death singing, says Thomas of Celano, summing up the impression of those who saw him then.

To be once more at Portiuncula after so long at the bishop's palace was not only a real joy to his heart, but the pure air of the forest must have been good for his physical well-being. He took advantage of this time to dictate his will.

In this record, which is of incontestable authenticity, the most solemn manifestation of his thought, the Poverello reveals himself absolutely, with candor, humility, and sincerity. His conscience proclaims here its sovereign authority: "No one showed me what I ought to do, but the Most High himself revealed to me that I ought to live conformed to his holy gospel."

When one speaks this way, submission to the Church is encroached upon. We may love her, hearken to her, venerate her, but we feel ourselves, perhaps without daring to admit it, superior to her. Let a critical hour come, and one finds oneself heretic without knowing it or wishing it. "Ah, yes," said Angelo Clareno, "St. Francis promised to obey the pope and his successors, but they cannot and must not command anything contrary to the conscience or to the Rule." For him, as for all of the spiritual Franciscans, when there is conflict between what the inward voice of God ordains and what the Church wills, he has only to obey the former.

Even today, thinkers, moralists, and mystics may arrive at solutions very different from those of the Umbrian prophet, but the method that they often employ is his. We may acknowledge Francis as the precursor of religious subjectivism. The Church immediately acknowledged as much. Four years after Francis dictated his last will and testament, perhaps to the very day (September 28, 1230), Ugolino, then Pope Gregory IX, solemnly interpreted the Rule—in spite of Francis's forbidding all commentary on it or his will—and declared that the Brothers Minor were not bound to the observation of the will.

Certainly the Church should be mistress in her own house. There would be nothing wrong if Gregory IX had created an order conformed to his views and ideas, but in this case, we can only feel a bitter sadness.

Upheld by the papacy, the Brothers of the Common Observance made the Spirituals sharply expiate their attachment to Francis's last requests. Caesar of Speyer died violently at the hand of the brother placed in charge of him. The first disciple, Bernard of Quintavalle, hunted like a wild beast, passed two years in the forests of Monte-Sefro, hidden by a woodcutter. The other first companions who did not succeed in flight had to undergo the most severe treatment. In the March of Ancona, the home of the Spirituals, the victorious party used terrible violence. Francis's will was confiscated and destroyed; they went so far as to burn it over the head of a friar who persisted in desiring to observe it.

Francis's Will—A Literal Translation

See in what manner God gave to me, Brother Francis, to begin to do penitence: When I lived in sin it was very painful to me to see lepers, but God led me into their midst and I remained there a little while. When I left them, that which had seemed bitter to me had become sweet and easy.

A little while later I left the world, and God gave me such a faith in his churches that I would kneel down with simplicity and say: "We adore you, Lord Jesus Christ, here and in all your churches that are in the world, and we bless you that by your holy cross you have ransomed the world."

The Lord also gave me and still gives me a great faith in priests who live according to the form of the holy Roman Church; because of their sacerdotal character, even if they persecuted me, I would return to them. And even if I had all the wisdom of Solomon, if I should find poor secular priests, I would not preach in their parishes without their consent. I desire to respect them as I do the others, to love them and honor them as my lords. I will not consider their sins, for in them I see the Son of God. I do this because here below I see nothing. I perceive nothing corporally of the most high Son of God except his most holy Body and Blood, which they receive and they alone distribute to others.

I desire above all things to honor and venerate these most holy mysteries and to keep them precious. Whenever I find the sacred names of Jesus or his words in indecent places I desire to take them away. We ought to honor and revere all the theologians and those who preach the most holy word of God, dispensing to us spirit and life.

When the Lord gave me some brothers, no one showed me what I ought to do, but the Most High revealed to me that I ought to live according to the model of the holy gospel. I caused a short and simple formula to be written and the lord pope confirmed it for me.

Those who presented themselves to observe this kind of life distributed all that they had to the poor. They contented themselves with only a tunic, patched within and without, with the cord and breeches, and we desired to have nothing more.

The clerics said the office as other clerics do, and the laymen said the Paternoster.

We loved to live in poor and abandoned churches, and we were ignorant and submissive to all. I worked with my hands and will continue to, and I will that all of the friars work at some honorable trade. Let those who have none learn one, and flee idleness. Let us resort to the table of the Lord, begging our bread from door to door. The Lord revealed to me the salutation that we ought to give: "God give you peace!"

Let the brothers take great care not to receive any gifts of churches, habitations, and all that people will build for them, except as in accordance with the holy poverty that we have vowed to in the Rule, and let them not receive hospitality except as strangers and pilgrims.

I absolutely forbid the brothers, in whatever places they may be found, from asking any bull from the court of Rome, whether directly or indirectly, under pretext of church or convent or preaching, nor even for their personal protection. If they are not received well somewhere let them go elsewhere, doing penance with the benediction of God.

I desire to obey the minister general of this fraternity and the guardian whom he may be pleased to give me. I desire to put myself entirely into his hands, to go nowhere and to do nothing against his will, for he is my lord.

Although I am simple and ill, I will, however, always want a cleric who will perform the daily office, as it is said in the Rule. Let all of the other brothers also be careful to do the office according to the Rule. If it comes to pass that any man does not perform the daily office, or desires to make changes to it, or is not Catholic, let the brothers bind him by obedience and deliver him to the minister. The minister shall guard him as a prisoner day and night until they have placed him in the hands of the Lord Bishop of Ostia, who is the lord, the protector, and the corrector of all the brotherhood.

Let the brothers not say: "This is a new Rule," for this is only a reminder, a warning, an exhortation. It is my will and testament, that I, little Brother Francis, make for you, my blessed brothers, in order that we may observe in a more catholic way the Rule that we promised the Lord to keep.

Let the ministers general, and all of the other ministers, be held by obedience to add nothing to and take nothing from these words. Let them always keep this writing near them, beside the Rule, and in all future chapters when the Rule is read let these words also be read.

I absolutely forbid by obedience all of the brothers from introducing commentaries to the Rule, or to this will, under the pretext of explaining it. Since the Lord has given me to speak and to write the Rule and these words in a clear and simple manner, understand them in the same way, and put them into practice until the end.

Whoever will have observed these things shall be crowned in heaven with the blessings of the heavenly Father, and on earth with those of his well-beloved Son and the Holy Spirit, with the assistance of all the heavenly virtues and all the saints.

And I, little Brother Francis, your servant, confirm to you so far as I am able this most holy benediction. Amen.

After thinking of his brothers, Francis thought of his dear Sisters of San Damiano, and he made a will for them. It has not come down to us, but in the last words that he addressed to the Sisters of St. Clare, after calling on them to persevere in poverty and union, he gave them his benediction. Then he recommended them to the brothers, reminding them never to forget that they are all members of the same religious family. After having done all that he could do for those whom he was about to leave, he was ready; he had finished his work.

Did he then think of the day when, cursed by his father, he renounced all earthly goods and cried to God with an ineffable confidence, "Our Father who art in heaven!"? We cannot say, but he desired to finish his life by a symbolic act that very closely recalls the scene in the bishop's palace.

Francis asked to be stripped of his clothing and laid on the ground. He wished to die in the arms only of his Lady Poverty. With one glance he embraced the twenty years that had glided by since their union: "I have done my duty," he said to the brothers, "may Christ now teach you yours!" This was Thursday, October 1.

They laid him back on his bed, and according to his wishes, they again sang to him the Canticle of the Sun. At times, he added his voice to those of his brothers, and also, he sang Psalm 142, that song of passionate hope:

> With my voice I cry to the Lord; with my voice I make supplication to the Lord.
> I pour out my complaint before him; I tell my trouble before him.
> When my spirit is faint, you know my way.
> In the path where I walk they have hidden a trap for me.
> Look on my right hand and see—there is no one who takes notice of me; no refuge remains to me; no one cares for me.
> I cry to you, O Lord; I say, "You are my refuge, my portion in the land of the living."
> Give heed to my cry, for I am brought very low.
> Save me from my persecutors, for they are too strong for me.
> Bring me out of prison, so that I may give thanks to your name.
> The righteous will surround me, for you will deal bountifully with me.

The hours flowed by and the brothers would not leave Francis alone. "Good father," one of them said, unable to contain himself any longer, "your children are going to lose you and be deprived of the true light for their way. Think of the orphans you are leaving behind and forgive all their faults; give to them all, present and absent, the joy of your holy benediction."

"God is calling me," replied the dying Francis. "I forgive all of my brothers their offenses and faults, and I absolve them according to my power. Tell them so, and bless them all in my name."

Then he laid his hands upon those who surrounded him. He did this with particular emotion toward Bernard of Quintavalle, saying, "I desire, and I urge with all of my power, that whoever shall be minister general of the Order will love and honor him as myself. Let the provincial ministers and all the brothers act toward him as toward me."

He had lost the notion of time. Believing that it was still Thursday, Francis desired to take a last meal with his disciples. Some bread was brought, he broke it and gave it to them, and there in the poor cabin of Portiuncula, without altar and without a priest, they celebrated the Lord's Supper.

Saturday, October 3, 1226, at nightfall, without pain and struggle, he breathed the last sigh. The brothers were still gazing on his face, hoping to still catch some signs of life, when larks alighted, singing, on the thatch roof of his cell, as if to salute the soul that had just taken flight. They gave the little poor man the canonization of which he was most worthy—the only one, doubtless, that he would ever have coveted.

The next day at dawn the Assisans came down to take possession of his body and give it a triumphant funeral. By a pious inspiration, instead of going straight to the city, they went around by San Damiano, and thus realized the promise made by Francis to the Sisters a few weeks before, to come and see them once more.

The brothers forgot their sadness on seeing the stigmata, and the inhabitants of Assisi showed an indescribable joy on having their relic at last. They deposited it in the Church of San Giorgio. Less than two years later, on Sunday, July 26, 1228, Pope Gregory IX came to Assisi to preside in person over the ceremonies of canonization, and to lay, the next day, the first stone of the new church dedicated to the one who bore the stigmata.

Built under the inspiration of Gregory IX and the direction of Brother Elias, this marvelous basilica is also one of the documents of this history, and perhaps I have been wrong in neglecting it. Go and look at it—proud, rich, powerful—

Francis's remains were buried in the new basilica in 1230, but the brothers concealed them extraordinarily well. Almost six hundred years later, in September 1818, Pope Pius VII gave his permission for a search to be undergone below the main altar of the lower church in the basilica.

Francis's tomb was discovered two months later; his remains were exhumed and a new crypt was built to house them. This crypt—directly beneath the lower church, which is directly beneath the upper church—is visited today by millions of pilgrims each year.

and then go down to Portiuncula, passing over to San Damiano, and hasten to the Carceri. You will understand the abyss that separates the ideal of Francis from that of the pontiff who canonized him.

Drawing of "The Basilica di San Francesco from the Plain," by Nelly Erichsen, reproduced from GORDON, p. 147.

FOUR TALES
FROM
THE LITTLE FLOWERS
OF ST. FRANCIS

1

The Source of Joy, or, Francis and Leo Walking in the Freezing Rain

One cold, wintry day Francis was traveling on foot with Brother Leo, one of his closest friends, to Santa Maria degli Angeli. Knowing that Leo was bothered by the cold and the freezing rain falling on them, Francis said, "Leo, although we may give sight to the blind, cause the deaf to hear, and even raise the dead—these things are not the source of perfect joy."

Confused and somewhat angry, Leo walked more briskly, leaving Francis further behind him. After another short while, Francis spoke loudly to Leo, "Brother, know that even if we know the scriptures by heart and have learned the words of the theologians— there is no perfect joy in that!"

Leo heard him, but walked even faster, pretending he hadn't. Soon, Francis shouted to him, "Leo, my friend, if we know the courses of the stars, and the virtues of all of the plants and herbs—these things will never be the source of perfect joy!"

For two miles, this went on. Finally, Leo stopped, turned quickly around, and said, "Francis, please—tell me the source of perfect joy!"

Francis replied, "When we arrive at our destination—our cloaks drenched by rain, our bodies shivering with cold, hungry and tired—and we knock at the door of our host asking to come in—if he then says to us, 'Wait outside until it is dark'—and if he then insults us, calling us thieves and perverts, and he tells lies to his neighbors about us so that they come and beat us, leaving us for dead—if we bear all of this with patience, kindness, and love—we will be brimming with joy. In self-conquest is perfect joy."

2

Francis Saves and Nurtures the Turtle-Doves

One day in the public square of Assisi, Francis encountered a young man with turtle-doves for sale. The boy told Francis that he had just caught them in the countryside, and Francis, with his tender love for all of God's creatures, felt sorry for the caged birds.

In addition to tenderheartedness, Francis was also eloquent of speech. He convinced the boy to give him the turtle-doves, saying, "I pray that you will give them to me, these birds that are so gentle, which holy scripture compares to chaste, humble, and faithful souls, so that they will not fall into the hands of cruel people intent on killing them."

The boy was won over and gave the creatures to Francis. Francis gathered them carefully into the lap of his frock and, walking slowly to Portiuncula, spoke softly to them, saying, "My dear sisters, simple-minded turtle-doves, innocent and chaste, why have you let yourselves be caught? I will keep you from some knight's table and make you nests, so that you will be fruitful and multiply, as our Creator commands."

So St. Francis went and made nests for them all, and after a short while the turtle-doves began to lay eggs and hatch them under the care of the brothers. The birds became so tame that it seemed that they had been fed by hand since the day of their birth. Meanwhile, Francis said to the boy who had given the turtle-doves to him: "My little son, you will be a brother in this Order and do precious work for Jesus." So it was, and the youth joined the Brothers Minor and lived in great sanctity with them all the days of his life.

After some time of their bringing joy to Francis, the brothers, and their Creator, Francis gave the turtle-doves his blessing to leave their cages, and they returned to the countryside.

3

How Francis Delivered a Brother
from the Hold of the Devil

One day in Portiuncula while at prayer alone in his cell, St. Francis saw a vision of the whole house surrounded and besieged by devils. They were like a great army surrounding the place, but none of them could gain entrance to the house. The brothers were so disciplined and devoted in their lives of sanctity that the devils were frustrated without a host upon whom they might find a way in.

It happened, in the days soon after Francis's vision, that one of the brothers became offended by another and he began to think in his heart of ways to revenge the slight. While the scheming brother was devising vengeful plans, entertaining wicked thoughts, the devil, finding an open door, entered Portiuncula upon his back.

Francis, the watchful shepherd of his flock, saw that the wolf had entered, intending to devour his little sheep. At once, Francis called the brother to him and asked him to disclose the hatred that had caused this disturbance in the house. The brother, frightened that Francis knew the content of his heart, disclosed to him all of the venom and malice that consumed him, acknowledging his fault and begging humbly for forgiveness.

Loving his sheep as does the Father, the shepherd soon absolved the brother, and immediately, at that moment, before his very face, Francis saw the devil flee from their presence.

The brother returned to the flock and the wolf was gone from the house.

4

When Francis and Rufino Preached in Their Breeches to the People of Assisi

It happened that Brother Rufino, one of Francis's closest companions, took to contemplation so much that, over time, he became almost mute in his love of God. He rarely spoke, and never preached as did the other brothers, for he spent all of his time in quiet meditation, absorbed in the Divine mysteries.

One day, Francis asked Rufino to go into Assisi and preach to the people as God inspired him. Rufino answered him, saying, "Reverend father, please pardon me and do not send me. I do not have the gift of preaching, but am only simple and ignorant."

"Since you have not obeyed as you should," Francis said sternly, "I command you, by holy obedience, to get yourself to the first Assisan church and preach to the people there. You shall stand before them naked as on the day you were born, wearing only your breeches."

At Francis's command, Brother Rufino stripped himself and walked to Assisi. He bowed in reverence to the altar of the first church he found and went up to the pulpit to preach. All of the people who saw him, and who assembled in the church to hear him, began to laugh. They said, "Look at how these men do so much penance that they become fools and are beside themselves!"

While Rufino was away preaching, St. Francis recalled Rufino's quick, holy obedience and the difficult commandment that he had put upon him. Francis began to scold himself, saying "How did you become so bold, you, son of Bernardone, vile wretch? Brother Rufino was one of the most noble gentlemen in all of Assisi before he joined your small order, and you sent him there to preach to the people like a madman?"

And so Francis immediately, then, stripped himself, as Rufino had done, and made his way to the church in Assisi where Rufino was preaching. Brother Leo traveled with him, carrying his tunic, and that of Rufino.

When the people saw Francis, they mocked him also. But Francis entered the pulpit, also clad only in his undergarments, and began to preach beautifully and eloquently on the subjects of voluntary poverty, holy penitence, and the right desire for the kingdom of heaven. He spoke also of the nakedness and shame of the passion of our Lord, Jesus Christ.

The people of Assisi were greatly moved on that day. Many devout and contrite hearts were won by the preaching of the two friars. On that day, so much did the devotion of the people increase for Francis, that they began to think themselves blessed if they could touch the hem of his garment.

A FEW NOTES ABOUT
THE EDITING OF SABATIER

Sabatier's *Life* of Francis, as presented here, has been edited and slightly abridged from the first English language edition of 1906, copyright renewed in 1938. Several guidelines have been followed such that would have been invisible to the reader unfamiliar with the first English language editions, but nevertheless, may be of interest to some.

First, grammatical choices have been occasionally updated to reflect contemporary English usage. For example, many uses of "shall" have been replaced by "will," "why" for "wherefore," "freedom" for "liberty," "brothers" for "brethren," and so on. Similarly, the spellings of some common names have been updated to reflect more common, Anglicized usage today: Joachim of Fiore to replace Sabatier's Gioacchino of Fiore, Sylvester to replace Silvestro, St. Clare replacing Santa Clara, and so on. On the other hand, a few proper names have been un-Anglicized, also in order to reflect more common usage today—replacing St. Damian with San Damiano, for instance. Sabatier and his English translator, Louise Seymour Houghton, made the semi-colon ubiquitous; many of these instances have been replaced with alternate punctuation.

In some cases, phrases and sentences have been refashioned. These changes are subtle and, hopefully, will serve today's reader in better understanding Sabatier's intent.

Some of Sabatier's exclusive masculine pronouns referring to all people have been quietly changed to a more inclusive alternative. Obvious typographical mistakes and inconsistencies have been corrected wherever possible.

Sabatier's scholarship was groundbreaking, in its time, but is today somewhat dated. Several cases of this have been excluded from the current edition; at least one other instance has been silently corrected: Clare was born of the noble family Offreduccio, not Sciffi, as Sabatier originally noted (BROWN, p. 326).

A substitute translation (the NRSV) has been given for quotes from the Hebrew or Christian Scriptures. Matthew Arnold's translation of "The Canticle of the Sun," quoted in full by Sabatier, has been retained, but with minor word changes consistent with those made to Sabatier's text as a whole. Selections from Dante's *Divine Comedy*, found in the annotations, are from the historic Longfellow translation.

In three instances, one of Sabatier's chapters has been divided into two, for the sake of length and context. The introduction and chapter fifteen of the original edition have been excluded completely, with the exception of a few quotes inserted as annotations within other chapters and in the editor's Introduction.

GLOSSARY OF TERMS

ACRE

St. Jean d'Acre, or Ptolemais, before it became an important, strategic city held by the crusader armies around 1100 C.E. They built a great fortress there, on the coast of the Mediterranean Sea, about fourteen miles north of Haifa. Visitors to Akko, as Acre is known today, may visit the "underground city" of old Acre; when the city finally fell to the Muslims in 1191 it was almost leveled to the ground.

ARNOLD OF BRESCIA

A fascinating Italian monk who was active as a reformer before Francis's birth (d. 1155). Told to confine himself to a monastery, he refused and spoke out against abuses in the Church of his day. He preached about the sanctity of poverty and even challenged the exclusive right of priests to administer the sacraments and hear confessions. Eventually, Arnold was hanged by the Roman authorities, with the blessing of the Church, and his ashes were scattered over the Tiber River so that his followers would not venerate his bones.

ATHOS

The famous Greek peninsula/mountain/monastic republic, often referred to as the "Holy Mountain," home to many communities, or sketes, of Orthodox Christian monks and hermits.

BULL

Official documents from the Holy See in Rome. The name comes from a Latin word which means "to boil." Both papal and royal documents were sealed distinctively with lead; a bull literally refers to the leaden seal on an official document.

CATHARS

Heretical movement that flourished in late medieval Europe, characterized by a distrust of the material world and a denial of Christ's humanity and bodily resurrection.

CHAPTER-GENERAL

A meeting of all members of an Order at which governing decisions are made.

CISTERCIANS

A monastic Order begun as a reform movement in 1098 in France. Its founders were intent on living more faithfully Benedict of Nursia's foundational Rule for monasteries. In the seventeenth century, two versions, or observances, became distinct within the Cistercians: common and strict (also called "Trappists," named for an abbey in France). Bernard of Clairvaux was an important early Cistercian. The popular spiritual writer Thomas Merton, of the 1940s to 1960s in America, was a Trappist.

CURIA

Leaders and other ministers who assist the pope in governing the Catholic Church.

ELIZABETH OF SCHÖNAU

Benedictine superioress at the monastery of Schönau, and friend of Hildegard of Bingen. Her book, Liber viarum Dei, *similar to Hildegard's better known* Scivias, *uses a prophet's fervor to remind readers to be faithful to Christ, to ward off worldliness (pointing out priests and monks for special admonition), and— foretelling the message of Francis—to put on the poverty and self-denial taught by Christ.*

HILDEGARD

Hildegard of Bingen (d. 1179), was a nun, mystic, and founder of convents, including one in Bingen on the Rhine River in Germany. She was the confidante of popes, kings, and theologians, including Bernard of Clairvaux and Pope Eugenius, who granted an imprimatur for her first, and most influential, visionary work, Scivias *("Know the Ways of the Lord").*

HUMILIATI

This odd group was an association of lay people who dressed plainly and practiced asceticism of various kinds, devoting themselves to charity. The Humiliati originated in Lombardy in the eleventh or early twelfth century. First approved by Innocent III in 1201, the Order witnessed the suppression of its male branch in 1571 by a papal bull after one of its leaders attempted to murder an emissary of Pope Pius V who was charged with reforming it.

MICHAELMAS

From a Middle English term literally meaning "Michael's Mass," September 29, the feast of Saint Michael the Archangel.

MISSAL

A book containing all of the texts that are read or sung during the mass through-out the year.

MENDICANT ORDERS

Mendicant literally means "a beggar." Three mendicant orders were founded as reform movements in the thirteenth century—Franciscans, Dominicans, and Carmelites—emphasizing a vow to personal poverty and begging alms.

POVERELLO

A name for Francis, meaning "little poor man."

SECULAR CLERGY

Those who are ordained but do not follow a religious rule (as monks do). They are similar to what today we most often refer to as parish priests, as opposed to mem-bers of religious orders.

SIMONY

To sell or buy spiritual things that should only be gained spiritually. The name derives from a character in the New Testament Book of Acts, Simon Magus, who was scolded by Peter for attempting to purchase the right to become an apostle (8:9–24).

WALDENSIANS

A reform movement from the twelfth and thirteenth centuries founded by Peter Waldo from the city of Lyons. The Waldensians, also called "the poor of Lyons," claimed to represent a true remnant who, from within, had been resisting the Catholic Church and attempting to reform it since the days of Constantine in the fourth century.

WHITSUNDAY

The feast of Pentecost, celebrating the "birthday" of the Church, when, according to the New Testament Book of Acts, the Holy Spirit first descended on the followers of Jesus after his Ascension into heaven.

SUMMARIES OF MAJOR CHARACTERS

ANGELO

One of Francis's closest disciples, co-author of The Legend of the Three Companions. Angelo Tancredi was of noble birth, from Rieti, and the first knight to join the Brothers Minor. He was with Francis for the Sermon to the Birds.

BERNARD OF QUINTAVALLE

Along with Leo and Masseo, perhaps the brother closest to Francis's heart. As he lay dying, Francis said of him: "I desire, and I urge with all of my power, that whoever shall be minister general of the Order will love and honor him as myself. Let the provincial ministers and all the brothers act toward him as toward me."

BONAVENTURE

The most important of the second generation of Franciscans (d. 1274). He wrote one of the early biographies of the saint and was elected Minister General of the Order in 1257 at the age of thirty-six. He was a rare combination of scholar, mystic, and saint, known for his great humility. Often referred to as "The Seraphic Doctor."

CAESAR OF SPEYER

Franciscan Brother recruited on Elias's mission to Syria. After Francis's death, in the fights between the defenders of the strict observance and Elias and the leaders of the Order, Caesar was imprisoned and beaten to death.

CLARE

The first woman to join Francis's movement after refusing to be married and completely dedicating herself to the ideals of the early Rule. One of Francis's closest friends, she lived beyond him more than twenty-five years. Two of her sisters— Agnes, who eventually became Abbess of a convent near Florence, and Beatrice— followed Clare in joining the Second Order, as did her mother, Ortolana, the year of Francis's death.

EGIDIO

One of Francis's first and closest disciples. Known for his zest for long, adventurous journeys. He is sometimes referred to as one of Francis's "knights of the round table." Co-author of The Legend of the Three Companions.

ELIAS

Early friend and follower of Francis (d. 1253). Francis appointed him Vicar of the Franciscan Order in 1221, and after Francis's death, he played a large part in Francis's rapid canonization and the building of the Basilica di San Francesco in Assisi. The incredible popularity of Assisi as a place of pilgrimage is owed, in large part, to Brother Elias. He was later deposed as a traitor to Francis's ideals and excommunicated, repenting of his arrogance on his deathbed.

GINEPRO

One of Francis's first twelve disciples and friends. A sustainer of the "Spiritual" movement, adhering closely to the original Rule, after Francis's death. His deeds of holy foolishness were appended to The Little Flowers, *and he was said to "delight in his own confusion."*

INNOCENT III

The pope who approved the formation and ministry of Francis's movement. One of the most important, powerful, and influential of late medieval popes. Elected at the age of 37, he ruled from 1198 to 1216.

JOACHIM OF FIORE

Former Cistercian abbot who became a mendicant reformer in the decades before Francis's conversion. His teachings and influence with his followers were similar to those of Francis. Declared a heretic by the Church.

LEO

One of Francis's closest disciples, co-author of The Legend of the Three Companions. *His occasional stubbornness adds humor to some of the stories in* The Little Flowers. *Nicholas Kazantzakis chose Leo as the narrator for his novel* Saint Francis.

MASSEO

One of Francis's closest companions. A tall, handsome, and intelligent man, Francis tested his humility by appointing him gatekeeper, almsgiver, and cook for the other brothers. He lived longer than most of the early companions of Francis, dying in 1280, more than fifty years after Francis's canonization.

PETER BERNARDONE

Francis's father, a merchant of fine linens, widely traveled. He loved luxury, probably because he had worked very hard to obtain it, and is represented in most biographies of Francis as an enemy of his son's best intentions to love Poverty.

PETER OF CATANA

The first Minister General of the Franciscan Order, installed by Francis himself. Peter led the friars for less than a year. His untimely death led to the period of Brother Elias's leadership.

RUFINO

One of Francis's closest disciples, a nobleman from Assisi, who gave up his worldly position and possessions to join the Poverello. Co-author of The Legend of the Three Companions.

SYLVESTER

The first priest to join the Brothers Minor (1210). Recognized in Franciscan tradition as one of the early contemplatives of the Order, living most of his religious life in a grotto at the Carceri.

THOMAS OF CELANO

An early Franciscan and Francis's first biographer. Known as the poet.

UGOLINO

Cardinal, papal legate, special counsel to Francis, and later, Pope Gregory IX, who presided over the canonization of St. Francis in 1228, only two years after the saint's death.

UGOLINO

Ugolino of Monte Santa Maria, from Naples (d. 1348) was a Spiritual Franciscan brother who compiled the collection of short tales from Francis's life and legend known as The Little Flowers of St. Francis *(I Fioretti di San Francesco, in Italian), first written in Latin sometime between 1330 and 1340 (under the title* Actus Beati Francisci et Sociorum Ejus*), approximately 110 years after the saint's death.*

SOURCES/RECOMMENDED READING

ALCORAN: Anonymous. *The Alcoran of the Franciscans, or a Sink of Lyes and Blasphemies*. London: 1679. Copy in the Sabatier Collection, Rare Books & Manuscripts, Boston Public Library.

ARMSTRONG: Armstrong, Regis J., J. A. Wayne Hellmann, and William J. Short, eds. *Francis of Assisi: Early Documents*. Vol. 1, *The Saint*. New York: New City Press, 1999.

ASSISI: "The Assisi Compilation." In *Francis of Assisi: Early Documents*. Vol. 2, *The Founder*. Ed. Regis J. Armstrong, J. A. Hellmann, and William J. Short. New York: New City Press, 2000.

BPL: Haraszti, Zoltan. "A Library about St. Francis." In *More Books: The Bulletin of the Boston Public Library*, Vol. VI, no. 7 (1931).

BROWN: Brown, Raphael, trans. *The Little Flowers of St. Francis: A Modern English Translation from the Latin and the Italian with Introduction, Notes, and Biographical Sketches*. New York: Image Books, 1958.

BURCKHARDT: Burckhardt, Jacob. *The Civilization of the Renaissance in Italy*. Trans. Middlemore. London: Phaidon Press, 1945.

BYNUM: Bynum, Caroline Walker. *The Resurrection of the Body in Western Christianity, 200–1336*. New York: Columbia University Press, 1995.

CAMILLE: Camille, Michael. *Image on the Edge: The Margins of Medieval Art*. Cambridge, MA: Harvard University Press, 1992.

CHESTERTON: Chesterton, G. K. *St. Francis of Assisi*. New York: Image/Doubleday, 2001.

COULTON: Coulton, G. G. *Medieval Panorama: The English Scene from Conquest to Reformation*. Cambridge, UK: Cambridge University Press, 1938.

COULTON 2: Coulton, G. G. *From St. Francis to Dante: Translations from the Chronicle of the Franciscan Salimbene, 1221–1288*. Philadelphia: University of Pennsylvania Press, 1972.

COWAN: Cowan, James. *Francis: A Saint's Way*. Liguori, MO: Liguori/Triumph, 2001.

CUNNINGHAM 1: Cunningham, Lawrence, ed. "The Vitality of the Franciscan Spirit: Reflections on the 750th Anniversary of the Death of St. Francis," *Christian Century*, October 13, 1976.

CUNNINGHAM 2: Cunningham, Lawrence, ed. *Brother Francis: An Anthology of Writings by and About St. Francis of Assisi*. New York: Harper & Row, 1972.

CUTHBERT: Cuthbert, Father, OSFC. *Life of St. Francis of Assisi*. New York: Longmans, Green, and Co., 1927.

DANTE: Alighieri, Dante. *The Divine Comedy*. Vol. 3, *Paradiso*. Trans. Henry Wadsworth Longfellow. Various editions.

DAVIES: Davies, Norman. *Europe: A History*. New York: Oxford University Press, 1997.

DEAN: Dean, Judith. *Every Pilgrim's Guide to Assisi and Other Franciscan Pilgrim Places*. Norwich, UK: Canterbury Press, 2002.

ECO: Eco, Umberto. *Art and Beauty in the Middle Ages*. Trans. Hugh Bredin. New Haven: Yale University Press, 2002.

ECO 2: Eco. Umberto. *The Name of the Rose*. Trans. William Weaver. New York: Harcourt Brace Jovanovich, 1983.

ELKINS: Elkins, James. *Pictures and Tears: A History of People Who Have Cried in Front of Paintings*. New York: Routledge, 2001.

FOLIGNO: Steegmann, Mary G., Trans. *The Book of Divine Consolation of the Blessed Angela of Foligno*. New York: Cooper Square Publishers, 1966.

GALLI: Galli, Mark. *Francis and His World*. Oxford: Lion Publishing, 2002, and Downer's Grove, IL: InterVarsity Press, 2002.

GEBHART: Gebhart, Emile. *Mystics and Heretics in Italy at the End of the Middle Ages*. Trans. Edward Maslin Hulme. London: George Allen & Unwin, 1922.

GOAD: Goad, Harold E. "The Dilemma of St. Francis and the Two Traditions." In *St. Francis of Assisi: 1226–1926: Essays in Commemoration with a Preface by Professor Paul Sabatier*. Ed. Walter Seton. London: University of London Press, 1926; pp. 129–162.

GORDON: Gordon, Lina Duff. *The Story of Assisi*. Illustrated by Nelly Erichsen and M. Helen James. London: J. M. Dent & Co., 1901.

GREEN: Green, Julien. *God's Fool: The Life and Times of Francis of Assisi*. San Francisco: Harper & Row, 1985.

HOLMES: Holmes, George. *The Oxford Illustrated History of Italy*. New York: Oxford University Press, 2001.

HOUSE: House, Adrian. *Francis of Assisi: A Revolutionary Life*. Mahwah, NJ: HiddenSpring/Paulist Press, 2001.

HUIZINGA: Huizinga, Johan. *Men and Ideas*. London: Eyre & Spottiswoode, 1960.

KAZANTZAKIS: Kazantzakis, Nikos. *Saint Francis*. Trans. P. A. Bien. New York: Ballantine Books, 1966.

KELLY: Kelly, J. N. D. *The Oxford Dictionary of Popes*. New York: Oxford University Press, 1988.

KOSSAK: Kossak, Zofia. *Blessed are the Meek: A Novel about St. Francis of Assisi*. Trans. Rulka Langer. New York: Roy Publishers, 1944.

MARTIN: Martin, Valerie. *Salvation: Scenes from the Life of St. Francis*. New York: Alfred A. Knopf, 2001.

MOORMAN: Moorman, John. *A History of the Franciscan Order: From its Origins to the Year 1517.* Oxford: Clarendon Press, 1968.

PARKS: Parks, George B., ed. *The English Traveler to Italy.* Stanford, CA.: Stanford University Press, 1954.

PARRY: Parry, Abbot, OSB, trans. *The Rule of Saint Benedict.* Herefordshire, UK: Gracewing, 1990.

RUNCIMAN: Runciman, Steven. *A History of the Crusades.* Vol. 3, *The Kingdom of Acre and the Later Crusades.* New York: Cambridge University Press, 1999.

SABATIER: Sabatier, Paul. *Life of St. Francis of Assisi.* Trans. Louise Seymour Houghton. New York: Charles Scribner's Sons, 1906, 1938.

SEDGWICK: Sedgwick, Henry Dwight. *Italy in the Thirteenth Century,* Vols. 1–2. Boston: Houghton Mifflin, 1912.

SETON: Seton, Walter, ed. *St. Francis of Assisi: 1226–1926: Essays in Commemoration with a Preface by Professor Paul Sabatier.* London: University of London Press, 1926.

SOURCEBOOK: Chaucer, Geoffrey. *Canterbury Tales.* Public domain modern translation, Internet Medieval Sourcebook; http://www.fordham.edu/halsall/source/CT-prolog-para.html.

THREE: "The Legend of the Three Companions." In *Francis of Assisi: Early Documents.* Vol. 2, *The Founder.* Ed. Regis J. Armstrong, J. A. Hellmann, and William J. Short. New York: New City Press, 2000.

WHICHER: Whicher, George F. *The Goliard Poets: Medieval Latin Songs and Satires.* New York: New Directions, 1949.

VORAGINE: de Voragine, Jacobus. *The Golden Legend: Readings on the Saints, Vol. II.* Trans. William Granger Ryan. Princeton: Princeton University Press, 1995.

INDEX